Survival Psychology

Escaping The Mind-Traps Of Survival Thinking
(The Leadership Guide)

TONY BROOKS

Endorsements

"This is a unique and groundbreaking book in the area of leadership mindset. This book provides a deep understanding of why and how our 'survival psychology' is such a strong force in modern life and how it can hijack us. This is a fascinating read and I highly recommend this to leaders at any level and across all sectors." - **Professor Paul McGee, Sunday Times Best Selling Author, The SUMO Guy**

"I wish I had read this book 10 years ago! A must read for any leader - I found so many lightbulb moments of "oh it's not just me who felt that way". This book is guaranteed to have an impact on your work and ultimately your happiness in life."- **Beth Bearder, Legal Director & Employment Lawyer at Halborns Law Firm**

"A clear, concise and helpful read for anyone interested in surviving the pressures of leadership. In fact, I would go so far as say, thriving is a better word. Well done Tony Brooks!" – **Dr Lynda Shaw, International Speaker, Neuroscientist and Leadership Psychologist**

"I would highly recommend this easily accessible, thought-provoking and practical book for Leaders which skilfully gives helpful advice, and space for self-reflection. Tony practically,

*yet sensitively, writes as someone with lived experience and expert professional knowledge."- **Dawn Wray, Gestalt Psychotherapist and co-founder of The Listening Collective***

*"I would recommend to any business leader out there, that they embrace the content of this thought-provoking book. Just when you think you are strong and polished in your own area of expertise, this book demonstrates that there is always a different way to manage and lead. It has made me think and re-evaluate my approach to leading my team and I will most certainly be trying out a number of the new working methods. A fantastic read." – **Karl Brooks, MD of Ti-Tek LTD***

"An insightful look into our present day behaviour and how our past can affect us, but doesn't have to hold us back. There are so many parts to this book I can relate to, and Tony has a fantastic way of grounding it in our working world and giving practical and useful advice and tools on how we can master our survival thinking for a happier more successful career." – **Helen Packham, Leadership Behaviour Specialist**

"For leaders grappling with self-doubt, witnessing negative behaviours in their peers, or looking to coach, mentor and develop future leaders in their teams, Survival Psychology is a must-read. The book provides useful insights into our psyche as well as practical tools to help control our primitive responses and enable us to fulfil much more of our potential as a leader." – **Iain Walker, Commercial Director, Ohme**

"Survival Psychology reveals with humour and wonderful real-life examples the enormous potential for living our best life. What shines through clearly is Tony's knowledge and deep understanding of the issues so many of us face in work and life. Gifting us not only an understanding of these areas from science, psychology and philosophy, but he also shares ideas and practices the reader can implement immediately. A great addition to anyone's book collection, if they are looking to master self-leadership and live the life that is truly available to them." - **Natalie Creasy, Little Soul Shack, Yoga Therapist, Advanced Meditator**

"Survival Psychology is a gem in the world of personal development and leadership. As a specialist in Leadership psychology, I was impressed by how Tony simplifies complex concepts of the human mind. He masterfully uncovers the ways we hinder our own progress and provides practical tools to break free from these limitations. This book is a must-read for anyone seeking to unlock their full potential and lead with wisdom and insight." – **Rachael Edmonson-Clark, Leadership Behavioural Expert, Professional Speaking Association President**

"Having worked closely with Tony over the years, I can honestly say this book is one you need on your desk – not just to read once but to refer back to over time. It's not just a book; it's a journey into the heart of what makes us tick and do the *things we do. Whether you're battling your own challenges or just fascinated by the power of the human mind, it gives us tools to better understand our behaviours so that we can respond positively and keep moving forwards. Tony has a knack for making complex ideas feel like a chat over a brew. I'm chuffed to bits to recommend this book – it's not just interesting – it's useful too." - **Charlie Whyman, B2B Marketing Strategist and MD of TGIS Aviation LTD***

"Survival Psychology by Tony Brooks is a game-changer for leaders navigating the modern jungle of challenges. In this insightful guide, Tony, a seasoned Leadership Psychologist and Coach, unveils the psychological traps that hinder growth - not just within leadership but for personal development too.

What sets this book apart is its immediate applicability. Tony doesn't just diagnose the problems; he provides practical tools and solutions to escape these mind traps. The standout chapter on ego is a gem, seamlessly blending insight and actionable advice.

I resonated with Brooks' conversational approach, making complex psychological concepts accessible without resorting to corporate jargon. The book focuses on leaders, but it would be incredibly useful to those aspiring to lead or simply wanting to 'be better' in their day to day approach to challenges, fears, and frustrations.

Survival Psychology is not just a read; it's a toolkit for leaders ready to conquer the psychological wilderness and emerge stronger than ever. Brooks' 17 years of experience and academic background in Psychology shine through, offering a unique and impactful guide for leadership growth." – **Colin Mobey, Team Development Consultant**

Acknowledgements

A big thank you to my wife Rebecca, for being the first proofreader of each chapter and for supporting me through the months of planning, writing, editing and publishing.

Thank you again to Taryn Lee Johnston, for taking me on again as a writer over 8 years since we worked on my first book together. Your patience and insights are as valuable now as they were before.

To my coach Helen Packham, I can't imagine ever not working with you. For all your guidance and support on my TEDx talk, my keynote and this book I am forever grateful.

My sincere appreciation goes out to all my test readers, for kindly sparing time on the run up to Christmas 2023 to provide much needed feedback:

- Professor Paul McGee
- Dr. Lynda Shaw
- Charlie Whyman
- Rachael Edmonson-Clarke
- Colin Mobey
- Karl Brooks
- Iain Walker

- Natalie Creasy
- Dawn Wray
- Beth Bearder
- Helen Packham

About the author

Tony Brooks is an experienced Leadership Psychologist, Coach, Author and recognised as an inspiring and impactful Keynote Speaker on Leadership Mindset and Survival Psychology.

Leadership Experience – He has over 20 years' experience as a leader and has been MD of his own company since 2007.

Track Record - Tony has worked with 1000s of leaders and teams, via 121 coaching, workshops, speaking and webinars. He has a proven track record of delivering personal growth, increased profit and positive company cultures.

Qualified Psychologist - Tony holds an MSc in Psychology.

Author – He is the author of 2015 book 'PI Leadership' – a 4.5 star rated book on Amazon.

TEDx Speaker – Tony is an experienced keynote speaker and a TEDx speaker on 'Unleashing You Creativity By Escaping Survival Thinking'.

Podcast – The 'Leadership Mindset' podcast series has been going now since 2018, with over 60 episodes.

Qualifications - An accredited member of the International Authority for Professional Coaching & Mentoring, The International Positive Psychology Association, Professional Speaking Association and was a 2016 finalist as Entrepreneur of the year in the East Midlands Chamber Business Awards.

Personal – Tony is married to Rebecca Holcroft-Brooks and has a daughter Thea, who is 25 years old at time of writing. In his spare time he is a keen music enthusiast, being a singer in a rock covers band and a huge Prince fan!

Table of Contents

INTRODUCTION

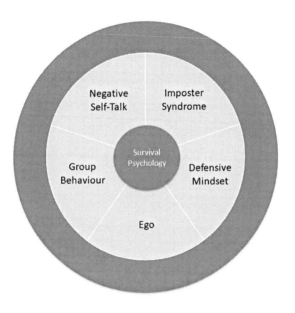

"Your survival thinking is continually on high alert, looking out for threats and in modern life these are not just physical but psychological in nature. It can often exaggerate, distort and imagine threats which don't even exist."

A trip to Edinburgh

In 2022, my daughter and I went on our annual 'Dad and Daughter' trip to Edinburgh. While we were there, we visited Camera Obscura, a house of fun and illusions. We both stood in front of mirrors that expanded us, distorted us and created images looking nothing like reality.

As a leader, this is what your survival thinking is doing to you every day. It's distorting threats, vastly exaggerating danger and imagining problems which don't exist.

It's like the mirrors in the fun house. But this experience is no fun for you at all!

Why did I write this book?

It's been 8 years since I wrote my previous book 'PI leadership – The 7 Positive Insight Steps To Peak Performance Leadership'.

After this amount of time (but still with the memory of all the hard work!), you may be asking what drove me to write this book? I've had a long-term fascination with psychology and mindset. It led me to study psychology to masters level, in addition to continually reading and researching. I've always wanted to gain a better understanding of my own psyche and others. This originates from my challenges over the years and battles with my own thinking. I've sought to gain a stronger perspective and control over some of the more destructive sides of my thinking.

Helping other leaders through these challenges is now very much the focus of my work and journey, in 121s, speaking, training and in my writing.

When I started to do my own research on books written about *survival psychology* and survival instinct, there were very few. We all need to be much more aware of what is going on with our thinking, why our *survival psychology* is holding us back on our leadership path and causing us so many challenges.

Why will you want to read this book?

Thank you for acquiring a copy of 'S*urvival Psychology*'.

I believe the reason you are reading this book is because you know you can perform at a higher level in your leadership position. You can tap into your potential in a much bigger way. I think you also know your internal psychology is your foundation and will ultimately determine your results as a leader.

I also believe you're reading this book because you're tired of things holding you back. You want to get a better understanding what is going on within your own psychology.

You want practical, easy ways to address the more destructive side of your thinking. Not complicated, long-winded approaches, but simple practical approaches. When your thinking is moving into those destructive areas you want to have methods to gain greater control over it. You want to do all you can to fulfil your potential as a leader and help others grow in their roles too.

Focusing too much on 'doing' things

As a leader, you will be spending way too much time focused on doing things. Your endless task list, resolving things which have gone wrong, emails hitting your inbox, fixating with business growth activities and daily actions. Yet the fundamental starting point is your own internal psychology.

Only by changing the quality of your thinking first will you be able to change your perspective. You will see yourself, your people and your organisation differently. Shifting your thinking and your perspective will enable you to do things differently and get better results. This book will help you do that.

The purpose of this book is to shift your thinking. I want you to understand how your *survival psychology* plays a much greater part in how you think and see your world than you believe. It's hijacking and trapping you on a daily basis.

Survival psychology

A number of years ago, I became fascinated with how our survival thinking can take over and trap us.

Firstly a definition:

"Survival psychology is the instinct and thinking which can take hold when we're driven by fear or the perception of threats to our safety, security or wellbeing. This may be in a physical sense or to our sense of self-esteem and psychological safety."

We go into survival mode quickly, often and mostly it's an overreaction. Our *survival psychology* exaggerates, distorts and imagines threats, just like those mirrors in Camera Obscura.

Survival thinking drives the well-known fight, flight or freeze response we can all encounter and respond with when picking up on perceived threats. It's vital in keeping us out of real danger. When someone is chasing you at night, a burglar is in your home or you're met with other threats, your survival instinct could be a matter of life or death.

But for the most part, your survival thinking will significantly overreact. It doesn't just want to keep you physically safe; it wants to keep you psychologically safe. It's unsettled by low levels of discomfort and will overcook these to be much bigger threats than they need to be.

Not feeling good enough

The more I've researched *survival psychology*, the more I realise one of the biggest challenges we face as a leader is battling with thinking which leads us to a place where we 'don't feel good enough'. Most of us are held back by this feeling. Over the past few years, I've gone deeper into why it's the case and why it presents such a challenge for us. I have come to the conclusion, through my research, that our survival instinct and survival thinking brings us to this place.

How we have evolved

If you go back to the African Savannah 2 million years ago, the origins of our Homo Sapien species were concerned with Sabre-Toothed Tigers attacking them (and hence the inspiration for the front cover!). The survival needs were more focused at the lower part of 'Maslow's Hierarchy of Needs' – on the basic needs for physical safety and security.

But in modern life, we still have a high level of anxiety and fear about things which could go wrong or threaten us. We're continually monitoring our environment for threats, but they are often more psychological in nature. These are more related to the higher part of 'Maslow's Hierarchy of Needs' – on the psychological and self-fulfilment needs for esteem, belonging and self-actualisation.

Our *survival psychology* turns inwards. We look for vulnerability and flaws in ourselves and threats to how the psychological needs will be met. We're constantly looking for where we're not good enough.

This might impact your personal life, or it could certainly be in your role as a leader.

Leadership and evolution

Leadership has been a fundamental part of our evolution, because we evolved and survived in groups. Within those groups, there was and still is a need for leadership. If we look far back to when we split away from apes, the genes passed on to us have necessitated certain behaviours which were dependent on the survival of our species. Many of those leadership tendencies still exist today. The elements which had an advantage in natural selection still ring true. Confidence, charisma, communication skills and being able to make decisions are still a key part of successful leadership.

We'll explore *group behaviour* in more detail later but, as a leader, your relationship with your survival thinking will impact how successful you are in your role. Your survival thinking can hijack you, but awareness and control will elevate your leadership performance. There are a number of matters to take on board, as you gain a deeper understanding of how your *survival psychology* plays out for you.

Being uncomfortable

The constant monitoring of our environments for potential issues, leads us to a place where we're exaggerating, distorting and even imagining problems. Some threats and dangers are real. But in many cases they aren't. They are just issues which will make us uncomfortable or unhappy. We've become too unaccepting of just being uncomfortable, as life will naturally do this for us at times.

Fear as a driving force

We're driven by fear. Fear for physical survival, but also fear for psychological, practical and financial survival in modern life. What could just be uncomfortable gets magnified. Emotion takes hold and our sense or perspective can be lost. If you've seen my TEDx talk, you'll know all about how I turned the loss of a tooth into a Sabre-Toothed Tiger! I made something that was relatively small in the grand scheme of things into something that was a much bigger adversity. A classic example of exaggeration driven by survival thinking.

The media and politicians know all about our *survival psychology*. They can use fear to sell a story, divide us or drive us to take the action they want.

When fear takes hold, it is hard to be rational. Even as a leader this can trip you up time and time again.

The battle between your potential self and destructive self

For many years I've used the concept of an internal battle which challenges leaders. The battle between the potential self (the incredible person we're capable of becoming) and our destructive self (the more destructive part of our psyche). Our fear and survival based thinking are prominent influences on the destructive self. They feed it and hold us back in many ways.

What's important is you become more aware of how your survival instinct can manifest and how you're then better able to manage it and realise more of your potential.

The biology of survival psychology

The brain has developed incredibly, over millions of years, in terms of size, and in terms of complexity (especially the cerebral cortex, the centre of rationale thought). Primitive parts of the brain and the emotional centre of the brain (as part of the Limbic System), still have a very strong impact in the way we process life. We have an incredible organ capable of amazing things, but it can also be our worst enemy.

The way we live our lives now, compared to 100,000 years ago or even 1,000 years ago, is vastly different. Our brain programming has evolved but it has not caught up. Our brains in modern life, attempt to make sense of an incredibly complex world, but with some primitive parts and thinking. As a leader you are dealing with a digital world that is advancing at an incredible pace!

Let's look at the physiology of what happens when we're either processing danger or perceiving potential danger. When perceived anxiety strikes (and our brain does not know the difference between real and imagined events) a series of physiological events occur which I'll summarise.

The amygdala (an emotional part of the limbic system and the centre of the defensive system) takes information on the perceived adversity or threats directly. This initially bypasses the cerebral cortex (the rational thinking part of the brain). It's what renowned Neuroscientist Jospeh LeDoux calls the 'quick and dirty route' and it's processed incredibly fast.

A chain of events is then set in motion. The amygdala then stimulates the SNS (Sympathetic Nervous System). There's a change in blood chemistry, where it coagulates and blood vessels are constricted. The heart and blood pressure increases. Adrenal glands secrete cortisol and adrenaline. Our field of sight is narrowed and our brain frequency increases, which reduces the functioning of our cerebral cortex and the ability for us to reason and think creatively. The result is we're hijacked psychologically and it takes place at an emotional level before rational thought can take hold.

The challenges leaders like you are facing

Over the past 3 years, I've spoken with many leaders, as part of my work as a leadership psychologist. I've had conversations with heads of companies, leaders within companies, HR managers, people in varying roles. I've gone out and presented and done keynote talks on this very topic.

Many leaders have shared with me how survival thinking has impacted them and their businesses and here are some examples:

"The biggest part of survival psychology I have witnessed, and seen in myself, is the 'giving up' which often happens when I'm pushed outside my comfort zone or into the unknown."

"In board meetings I don't understand all the figures and question; what am I doing here?"

"I put on a mask at work and then went home to throw up!"

Often, we don't share what is going on for us internally, as we fear how we will be judged. All these examples are not exceptional in my experience. It's a tragedy that many leaders, like you, battle with these kinds of internal challenges alone, when they could discover insights by talking about them more and gaining a shift in thinking.

In a broader sense survival thinking can impact you in your leadership role in these ways:

- How you react and make important decisions
- Your relationships with people across the business and especially in your teams
- Your confidence levels and self-belief
- The culture and behaviour of your team or organisation
- The performance, not only of you as a leader but the people you lead
- Most importantly it will impact on the results achieved by you and your teams

Stress and burnout (a state of emotional, physical and mental exhaustion) are widespread amongst senior leaders:

- 1 in 14 UK Adults feel stressed every day
- 1 in 5 feel stressed more days each month than they don't (CIPHR, 2021)

According to a new survey more than half of UK SME owners polled said they have experienced burnout since the start of the pandemic in 2020, which equates to around 2.9 million business owners across the UK suffering from burnout (FreeAgent, 2021).

The quality of your thinking will directly relate to how you see your world, your feelings and reactions. The problems with stress start fundamentally with how you think and improving the quality of your thinking is paramount. Being aware of and managing your survival instinct and thinking is a fundamental part of this.

We're losing people and work days due to the epidemic of stress and anxiety too:

- The staff turnover rates in the UK are approximately 15% per year. 4.1% days are lost through sickness
- Anxiety, stress, depression and other related illnesses are the most common reasons, accounting for 439,000 days lost
- It can cost £2-3000 to hire the average new employee, £4-10,000+ for more senior positions (NHS, 2021)

Your world

You are no doubt experiencing a number of challenges as a leader:

- It could be mounting stress and overwhelm
- It could be problems with remote work
- It could be problems with your people's behaviour and getting the best out of your people
- It could be difficulties making decisions

- It could also be the constant worry or anxiety about the future and not getting the right results

What will help you is to look under the hood to find out what is really going on with your thinking. Because only through being clearer and more aware of what's going on with your thinking, will you start to create more personal power, more power as an individual to do something about it.

Throughout this book, I'm going to give you some thoughts and ideas on strategies, techniques and approaches. We're also going to look at some examples from my conversations and time with leaders.

There are certain positions and situations which can significantly trigger the mind-traps of *survival psychology*:

Accidental Leaders	A leader has fallen into the position, either through being highly skilled and then promoted or heading up a company from the start (a 2013 CMI survey found as many as 82% of new managers in the UK fall into this category, with no formal training in leadership).

New Senior Leaders	Promoted to a higher leadership position, especially C-Suite position, where there is significant self-examination of suitability for the role.
Leaders going through grievance	One or more in the team have raised a formal grievance.
Leaders going through performance management	Leaders assessed to be underperforming in their role.

The 5 mind-traps of survival psychology

The aim of this book is to examine how your *survival psychology* can show up in 5 different ways and how the mind-traps of survival thinking can cause problems with your thinking as a leader or a senior business person.

Throughout, I want to help you become more aware of how your *survival psychology* manifests and for you to be able to manage it better, so it doesn't trap or hijack you!

As we go through all 5 of the areas of my *survival psychology* model in more detail, my aim for you is to gain an improved understanding of why your survival thinking takes such a dominant role in the way you process life. It will then lead you to an understanding of how it can manifest in those 5 different areas, which gives you the ability to make conscious choices and make decisions.

We're believed to be the only species (due to our vastly superior developed cerebral cortex) capable of rising to a higher level of consciousness, about our own thoughts. It's our superpower, if we choose to use it!

We will always have an element of thinking driven by our need for survival. We will always have the potential to be hijacked in those 5 ways driven by our *survival psychology.* Our personal power comes from accepting a greater element of discomfort in life and being much more conscious about the way we process what is going on and our thoughts and perceptions, so we can move to a more rational place and make the right choices for ourselves.

Let's introduce the 5 areas of *survival psychology.*

Impostor Syndrome

The first of these is the belief you may have *impostor syndrome.* The term *impostor syndrome* first originated from Dr. Pauline Clance and Dr. Suzanne Imes, who coined the term "impostor syndrome" when they published "The Impostor Phenomenon in High Achieving Women:

Dynamics and Therapeutic Intervention" in 1978. They defined this as "an internal experience of intellectual phoniness."

I define *impostor syndrome* as "the belief you will be found out as a being incapable of doing what you need to do and uncovered as a fraud."

Being found out in this way can happen in work and personal life and relates back to the core feeling of 'not being good enough'.

The experience of feeling an impostor can become especially apparent when I've spoken with people where they have been promoted or moved into new positions, particularly moving into senior leadership positions. An event of this nature triggers a psychological reaction where our psyche starts to look for potential flaws where we don't have the skills and where we fear we will be found out. Through many conversations I found many leaders have experienced this challenge on more than one occasion through their career path.

Defensive Mindset

The second area of the *survival psychology* model, which has come out of my research, is where people move into a *defensive mindset*. People can build a protective wall or a protective bubble around them to keep themselves safe. However, it will cause problems for them and others. It will limit their growth and their potential and is particularly triggered, where mistakes are made, when people are given critical feedback, or when challenges feel threatening. People can go into their shell, or they can come out fighting because they feel they need to defend their self-esteem and their sense of self. Much of this is about keeping us in our comfort zone and not facing up to an element of discomfort which is an important part of our growth.

Ego

The third area of my *survival psychology* model relates to the *ego* and the constant need to increase or prove our importance. *Ego* can be a truly damaging force in organisations and personal life. It can be damaging for individuals, with the constant need to compare and compete with others, to criticise others (and oneself) and to complain about your position. Our *ego* can be damaging to ourselves because it can keep us separate and avoid the connection which is important as part of being human.

It's also damaging to relationships with others, especially when you've got somebody who is very engulfed in their *ego* at the top of an organisation or heading up a team. You may well have seen leaders in organisations whose *ego* has caused a considerable amount of damage.

Group Behaviour

In the fourth area of the *survival psychology* model, we will take a look at *group behaviour*. We're group or pack orientated at our core. We fear isolation and need to connect with others. *Group behaviour* can be a force for problems, but it can also be a force for good.

Within organisations, the negative side can manifest in a number of ways. There can be a feeling the management are detached from the individuals within the organisation, with the resulting perception of an 'us and them' culture. We can also experience 'silo mentality', where teams don't cooperate or collaborate, but look to compete or become too defensive. People start pointing fingers and point scoring against other teams within the organisation. They look within to preserve the identity of the team, over and above the identity of the organisation.

Group behaviour is at the root of the human species and it can also be an incredible force for good. I've seen some brilliant examples within organisations, where there's been great work done on the culture. Collective work on the purpose and values, in unifying people with consistent behaviours. The outside world sees and understand this as the positive identity of the organisation. This is *group behaviour* at its best.

Negative Self-Talk

The fifth and final area is the continual *negative self-talk* we all indulge in. We have thousands of thoughts every day and this is a phenomenal amount of thinking. It's also been found that the majority of these thoughts are either doubtful or negative in nature and driven by our *survival psychology*.

We're very much 'thinking' beings. We're often gripped in an endless monologue of self-talk. The monologue can often be very unproductive and lead us to a really destructive state of mind. It leads us to think more pessimistically, very much driven by the need to keep ourselves safe. Our thinking is continually focused on monitoring our environment, looking to keep us safe, to ensure we don't expose our vulnerability.

How the 5 areas interrelate

It's important to accept and acknowledge the 5 areas don't exist in isolation. Through the book you will find the lines are blurred. *Ego* can play out collectively in group behaviours. *Impostor syndrome* is very much about protecting the *ego*. *Defensive mindset* can impact relationships between groups of people. *Negative self-talk* runs through all areas.

They are separated to give you greater understanding and to focus in on the area(s) tripping you up most. As you read this book, you may well find what you believed was your biggest challenge out of the 5 areas of *survival psychology* shifts and you start to see another area being more dominant for you. Go with the flow through the book, as it will no doubt be a mix of all 5 areas that bring you challenges.

Managing your survival psychology

The foundational drive for this book is to enable you to raise your awareness and gain greater understanding of how your survival thinking works. Your success, fulfilment and happiness as a leader need this.

It's not about "Feeling the fear and doing it anyway". It's more important to "Understand the fear first and then move forwards".

Practical tools and actions for you

You will still want practical solutions and I respect this completely.

Through all my work, I've examined ways to address the challenges faced by the mind-traps in all 5 of those areas. Through examining the challenges of leaders over the years, I've put together a range of tools and approaches to deal with the challenges you face when your *survival psychology* is wreaking havoc and hijacking you.

STRONG RECOMMENDATION – When you look at the tools in each of the 5 areas you may feel overwhelmed. I advise you pick only 1 or 2 to work on at a time. Select the 1 or 2 tools for each area you feel addresses your biggest challenges and focus on these first.

We will now go into all 5 areas in much more detail.

1. IMPOSTOR SYNDROME

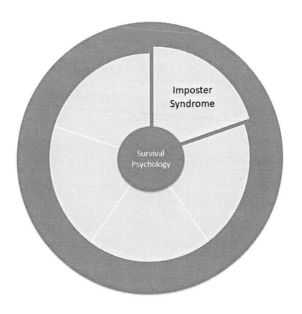

"You are not a fraud, you have a normal survival driven doubt that you are not good enough"

Do you think you have impostor syndrome?

This chapter on *impostor syndrome* may well be the one you felt drawn to most initially. I meet numerous leaders who believe they are impacted by *impostor syndrome* and it's often an early talking point in my 121 work. However, I have an important message for you! You may feel you have *impostor syndrome*, but one of my main aims is to reassure you that you don't have the syndrome at all.

Many leaders, like you, face challenges in their position. Often challenges relating to a lack of confidence which they attribute to a belief they have *impostor syndrome*. This has become more and more prevalent in the past 5 years, even though the term has been around since the 1970s.

The feeling of being an imposter can be damaging to established leaders, or new leaders and people moving into new positions. It may also be detrimental personally - in relationships and in the role of being a parent. It can create problems with anxiety, depression or hold you back from fulfilling your potential even remotely.

We are wired to seek the approval and validation of others from an early age. If we feel we are not getting this or not worthy of it, the impostor feelings come in. We need to understand it, its root causes and how we can gain control over it.

Definitions and interpretations

"Impostor Phenomenon" was first described by Pauline Rose Clance and Suzanne Imes, from observations in a clinical setting conducted in 1978. Their initial studies looked at a cluster of psychological disturbances in 150 highly successful women at Georgia State University. They defined individuals with "Impostor Phenomenon" as experiencing intense feelings that their achievements were undeserved and worried they are likely to be exposed as a fraud. Clance and Imes also describe the phenomenon as when a person feels their achievements are due to luck and not to their qualities and qualifications.

Another definition of "Impostorism", from Harvey and Cuts in 1985, states it as a psychological pattern rooted in intense concealed feelings of fraudulence, when faced with achievement on tasks and the inability to attribute own achievement to internal qualities, such as ability, intelligence or skills.

Impostor syndrome is not recognised as a medical condition

It's however important to note *impostor syndrome* is not recognised as a medical condition, both in relation to the International Classification of Diseases (ICD) and the Statistical Manual of Mental Disorders (DSM).

50 years on since the term originated, numerous leaders in modern life believe they clearly have some of the psychological disturbances associated with the term *impostor syndrome*. It's also found to be more prevalent in women. In fact, in a 2019 study by Clare Josa, 52% of women reported they have struggled with *impostor syndrome* on a daily or regular basis, compared with 49% of men. There are many situational and environmental aspects which impact on women with regards to this though and they need to be addressed by men.

Feeling an impostor is still a significant problem across both genders and the true numbers may well be higher, as self-disclosure can be uncomfortable. When I work 121 with leaders in a confidential relationship, *impostor syndrome* often comes up early on as a perceived issue.

Whilst it's not healthy for anyone to be labelling themselves with a syndrome (especially when the 2 major classifications do not see it as a medical condition), the underlying problem is something real people face on a regular basis. It's especially the case for individuals stepping into leadership roles or more senior positions for the first time.

The impact of survival thinking

People are impacted by the fear of being found out to be a fraud and the continual belief achievements are down to luck and so frequently end up doubting themselves. Promotions can increase these feelings considerably. You step up into a new position and fear you don't possess the right skills and characteristics to lead at this level and will be found out.

Ultimately, these fears of being found out are driven by survival thinking. Our survival thinking can go inwards as we have explored before, looking for flaws and vulnerability means we end up in a place where we do not feel good enough. Unfortunately, it's common for us all and a fundamental part of the human condition.

As human beings, we monitor our environment to keep ourselves safe. We are continually looking for problems, threats and dangers. As well as looking externally, we look internally and this can hijack us. Our fear of being found out or not being good enough can be strong and stop us attempting to understand what is going on and questioning it.

6 characteristics of feeling an impostor

The feeling of being an impostor can show up via 6 underlying characteristics, as described by Rose Clance in 1985. These are:

The impostor cycle	Leaders over prepare and put too much effort in to avoid being found out. They then discount positive feedback leading to a downward spiral on the next task.
The need to be special	Leaders in organisations set themselves incredibly high targets to prove themselves, but continually dismiss their talents and conclude they're stupid when they are not at their best.
'Super Person' Aspect	An even more exaggerated version of the need to be special.
Fear of Failure	Leaders who feel they are struggling with *impostor syndrome* tend to overwork to be certain they will not fail. Overworking impacts leaders, with the mounting problems of overload and stress which are often self-generated.
Denial of competence	No matter how much positive feedback a leader receives or the objective evidence of their competence, it will be discounted.

Guilt about success	Guilt can be triggered, especially when success at the level the leader has achieved is unusual in the family. It can lead to people feeling less connected and more distant and they could be overwhelmed by guilt about being different to friends and family.

You may well relate to one or more of these characteristics and find they hamper you in your role as a leader or in life in general. There are some common themes here:

- Overworking to prove yourself
- Setting very high standards
- Discounting positive feedback and results
- Poor self-image
- Guilt about success

Whether triggered by a syndrome or not, these are real experiences faced by almost all leaders at some time or another.

Impostor moments

Although the experiences feel very real, it's apparent there is no universal agreement this is a medical condition or a syndrome which is consistently recognised and understood. There are many different interpretations.

We all experience moments when we fear we may feel vulnerable and worry about being found out. It's part of our *survival psychology* as a human being. These feelings are in fact on a continuum from occasional worrying to continual worrying.

The feeling of being an impostor is not prevalent across all situations. It may well be a specific situation or environment which triggers your feelings. This can be different from work to personal life and also within different aspects of both those fields. In some areas of your leadership role you may well feel confident (maybe the more technical aspects), but in other aspects much less so (people leadership perhaps). Certain moments will then trigger the feeling of not being good enough or a fraud as a leader, leading to the belief you have a syndrome. You may well have found yourself attaching to this label, as it has become more and more common in later years.

It's critical to realise there are specific situations, environments and moments which trigger this feeling. For almost everyone it's not all encompassing, but happens based on certain triggers. We all have 'impostor moments' where we don't quite feel good enough. It's normal and you will find stepping into leadership positions will influence this greatly.

Be mindful too of comparing how you feel inside to how you see other leaders and people present externally. The belief others are more confident and not struggling with the same emotions you are having is a fallacy. Their inner feelings will no doubt include some of the same challenges you experience on occasions. We have more in common under the surface than we may believe.

The biology of feeling an impostor

When we look at the science of this, we are continually scanning for threats and dangers. The emotional centre of our brain (the amygdala) takes information directly from our senses, bypassing the rational thinking part of our brain (the cerebral Cortex). It's what neuroscientist Joseph LeDoux calls the 'quick and dirty route' and it happens incredibly speedily (this will be a common theme we return to through the book). We are triggered emotionally by potential adversity and this can be external, but it can also be internal.

Our emotions and fears overpower us. We can continually misinterpret the signals of modern life by exaggerating, distorting or imaging threats. We look inwards for vulnerability, weakness, fallibility and for ways in which we may be exposed. All this happens at such a level and so consistently, we can end with a default position of not feeling good enough. Not good enough as the head of a company, a leader, a parent, a spouse, a friend, a child. Not good enough in a whole multitude of roles, both professional and personal. This is the true underlying challenge of feeling an impostor.

The impact on your performance and other people within your organisation

Let's look further at Clare Josa's study to examine the impact on people's performance. The study found:

- 56% of people have not spoken up with ideas because of concerns about exposing themselves
- 25% turned down opportunities they wanted
- 35% didn't put themselves forward for promotions or awards because of the fear they would be found out to be a fraud or not good enough in the position

For leaders on their career path this can be very damaging and hold them back and I continually see examples of all the above in my work. It means the light inside does not get a chance to shine, potentially stifling the growth of leaders. It keeps them fixed in their current position and patterns of behaviour.

Impostorism as a form of bias and limiting belief

Impostorism or *impostor syndrome* is also a form of cognitive bias. It's a way of processing the world which is distorted. We can often build a negative view of ourselves and then look for evidence to support this view. Within this position a leader can experience cognitive dissonance, where who they believe they are is different to who they believe they should be.

We often operate with limiting beliefs. Leaders can hold tightly to the belief they are not good enough, even when the objective evidence says otherwise. Beliefs are hard wired into our neurology over time and are then difficult to re-wire. Beliefs will then be a big influence on our behaviour. They also impact on how we process new information. If the information does not fit our belief, it can be discounted. If it confirms our limiting belief that we are not good enough, it will be accepted to confirm this view. Updating your beliefs will need continual vigilance and work, but it can be done.

Confirmation bias is at play here, as it can reinforce the feeling of being an impostor and can uphold unsupportive beliefs. Confirmation bias is where we look for information to support a belief already held. As described, we monitor for evidence to confirm our impostor view of self.

The mind-traps leaders face with impostor syndrome

I've heard many direct examples of *impostor syndrome* playing out for leaders through time:

- Concerns about the views and opinions of others, including those expressed on social media
- Embarrassment of not knowing what they feel should be known
- Public speaking fears
- Feeling separate or different to other people in a group via one's race, gender identity or sexuality
- Being part of a senior team and not understanding the financials
- Being promoted to lead more people and not knowing how

Leaders can be uncomfortable sharing these kinds of thoughts with others in the organisation. They may feel more comfortable to do this in a 121 session with me or during a confidential call. The problem is that holding back supports the myth that we are alone when battling with these challenges. I'm sure you may well relate to one or more of the real-life examples above? Every leader will battle with one or more of these and it can be hard to resolve them alone. It's important we are all more bold in sharing our challenges and experiences.

Let's examine where the belief you are an impostor can impact your performance as a leader in certain scenarios.

Moving to a new leadership position

The feeling of being an impostor can be especially triggered when leaders move to a new position in an organisation, they find themselves leading people for the first time, they change companies or get promoted to a more senior position.

I have worked with leaders who have moved into C-Suite or Director roles, where most people would assume they take this in their stride, but often this is not the case. The need to operate at a higher level, be more strategic, lead a larger group of people and understand the complexities of company governance can all create internal doubts.

As with these examples, when moving to a new position you may well find yourself examining the ways in which you don't quite match up to the job spec of the particular role or the person who was in the role before you.

If you are leading people for the first time, you may well be unequipped for one of the most challenging aspects of work life. You will be concerned about the trust and respect people in your team will have for you.

I've been through this experience myself and worked with many leaders who have made this move. They've performed well technically in their role and so are promoted to lead people. This is a whole new skill that cannot just be picked up 'on the job'.

The feeling of being an impostor is very often when we take a step out of our comfort zone and being promoted is definitely a scenario when this can happen for us. We experience discomfort because we must deal with change or something new.

Being an accidental leader

If you are a CEO, owner or senior leader who's never had leadership development, this can also trigger a feeling of not being worthy or equipped for the position you find yourself in. You may have ended up in this position due to setting up the business from the start and the business developing and evolving around you over time.

You may feel you are getting by based on intuition and instinct and just practical experience. All of this is good but can lead to the feeling you've arrived at the place where you're now the owner of a larger business but concerned you're not really a proper business owner (a statement I've heard on more than one occasion). You are worried this will be found out. Not necessarily discovered by your people but as a result of the business failing because you're not worthy or don't have the skills needed to continue to grow the business. Nobody expects the person at the top to doubt themselves in this way, but I know firsthand that many do.

This situation often arises when individuals are elevated to leadership roles for their technical prowess and past accomplishments. Unexpectedly, they find themselves at the helm of senior team meetings, feeling unprepared. Numerous organisations fail to provide the necessary investment in these emerging leaders or to foster their skills in managing people. However, those enterprises that do commit to leadership development and support are the ones that truly reap the rewards of their personnel's capabilities.

Self-doubt and criticism

At the core of those scenarios is an inner fear of not being good enough. This can lead to you doubting your skills, abilities, competence and even character. It can also drive self-criticism for falling short of your high standards of validation or what you feel is expected by others. Addressing this can motivate you to work harder and demonstrate your capabilities. You continually set the bar higher to validate your abilities, so the doubt will persist and you will feel a fraud in the position you are trying to prove yourself.

As I've described before, the position of 'not feeling good enough' is based on evolutionary survival mentality and is wired into our neurology. Fear based thinking worked well when our radar worked to keep us physically safe, but in modern life this goes internal and makes us continually look for vulnerability or fallibility.

Self-doubt is normal and the more we normalise it (and talk about it) the easier it will be to gain a more helpful perspective. An element of self-doubt can be healthy, if coming from a firm foundation of self- worth. Seeing where we can improve is mature and rational. It's part of our journey of growth.

Self-sabotage

Leaders can self-sabotage to hold themselves back and keep out of 'threatening' positions. This will mean not going for those promotions, not making a move to a new company, or just not speaking up about your ideas. All these examples of self-sabotage or not valuing yourself can leave you stuck where you are. You fear being exposed and found out, so you stay put and keep quiet. Ultimately this will sabotage your path of growth through your career.

Overwork and perfectionism

Leaders impacted by *impostor syndrome* may well get gripped by perfectionism or expertism, because of the continual need to raise the bar to prove ourselves and try to address the feeling of not being good enough (the real underlying problem relating to feelings associated with *impostor syndrome*).

Nothing in life is perfect. Nothing you do will be perfect. Overworking and aiming for 100% in one area will impact on others. You will more often fall short across the board if you aim for perfection in one area.

I once worked with a female Business Development Manager who strove for excellence in tasks. The problem was that aiming for perfection in 1 out of 5 tasks meant that, although the first task was done incredibly well (probably more than needed!), she didn't get to the other 4 tasks in a timely manner and this meant they were either neglected or done last-minute with much stress.

Overworking across all areas is unsustainable and will cause big problems at some point. The need for perfection is a fallacy in almost all cases. It limits focus, distracts from other areas and leaves you feeling continually unfulfilled and unhappy. Perfectionism comes with great personal costs.

Perfectionism can also lead to you applying super high standards for others that can have a number of consequences. It can leave people feeling inferior or de-motivated as nothing seems to be good enough for you. Their own *impostor syndrome* can be triggered by your behaviour. It can also mean that you don't delegate for fear that things won't be done to your standards and this leaves you with too many tasks to deliver at too high a level.

Avoidance and procrastination

The flip side to overwork and perfectionism, is people can avoid doing things, believing that if they don't do something they can't fall short of the high standards they have set for themselves and they won't expose themselves to being found out. This is fundamentally driven by a fear of failure. They will procrastinate as this will, again, avoid the position of falling short or taking risks. It's ironic, as they ultimately fall short in a far greater way than if attempts had been made.

Failure and mistakes are not seen as a normal or healthy part of life when in this mindset, but they are seen as further evidence of the impostor belief of not being good enough.

I recognise that you may well prefer to work in a way that leaves things until late-on or the last minute. This may be your default way of working. It may not be down to fear-based procrastination. Again, I have senior leaders who let me know this is their preferred and in-built way of doing things. Just be mindful of the increased stress levels of working in this way.

Also, sometimes delaying decisions is wise, it's not procrastination. It becomes problematic when it's persistent across many areas. There are risks in deciding or taking a path, but not making a decision is risky too!

People pleasing

People pleasing is another manifestation of feeling like an impostor. Again, this is driven by a default position of not feeling good enough. People pleasing can be seen in attempts to impress a senior manager or members of the team. It can also be shown when someone feels the need to agree too readily. If we please others, they are less likely to see or speak about us negatively. The need to please others may well be more heightened for some through childhood experiences.

Freeze (or Flop)

More extreme than avoidance, is freezing. Freezing is one of the 5 Fs of survival thinking – Friend, Fight, Flight, Freeze or Flop. We are gripped by fear and anxiety, so we become immobilised, both physically and psychologically. At the extremes this can lead to another F of survival – Flop. This comes into operation when 'Freeze' has been unsuccessful and this is when the mind and body shutdown.

Closing down like this can take the form of a mental breakdown and coming to a grinding halt. There are a number of people I've met through my life and work who have had total breakdowns, due to feeling overwhelmed and the stress of pushing themselves to be worthy in their role, for it to significantly impact on their health. If you are on this path, you need to take yourself off it using the right help and support.

Self-deprecation and guilt

As touched on for the 6 characteristics of *impostor syndrome* from Pauline Rose Clance, people who move into senior positions can be self-deprecating, because they won't want to appear they are in any way elite to others. This can be particularly associated with the guilt of success compared to colleagues, family members and friends. If you are the first in your family to reach this level, it can feel uncomfortable. If your progress moves you away from the colleagues and friends you have at work, this too can cause guilt and unease. Working to address this is important so it does not become more toxic for you.

Isolation

Many of the scenarios and problems discussed will lead people to become and feel more isolated. The situations can do this, but the internal feelings can be isolating too, especially for people who are more introverted in nature. It means they go inwards, they don't want to talk about the challenges they face, so they deal with them alone.

In my experience, being the head of a company or holding a leadership position can be a lonely place. It is hard to share feelings and insecurities with your people and you don't want to share it at home. But finding someone you can trust to confide in can provide an objective sounding board to support you on your journey. This can be a coach, leadership psychologist, mastermind group or someone in a similar position to you who you trust.

Mental health, depression and anxiety

Closing down in the ways described can then subsequently lead to further problems with stress, anxiety and with depression. Research in 2001 by Sonnak and Towell, found a high level of impostor fears were associated with poor mental health. A moderately strong correlation was found between impostor fears and mental health issues by the General Health Questionnaire in a sample of 117 undergraduate students.

The origins of challenges with impostor syndrome

Family and other influences can create challenges for people through time, leaving a lasting feeling of not being good enough and the feelings of being an impostor. The things said by a boss, a teacher or a parent in earlier years can be held onto throughout life. These can be deep rooted and may require professional therapy, but we also have a conscious choice in how we process these and the lessons we take away.

We have greater control over our self-image and self-beliefs than we might at first think, but there are a number of mindset shifts and actions which can help with the various challenges we have covered in this book.

How to escape the mind-traps of impostor syndrome

* Mindset

Firstly, we need to go back to the concept of 'understanding the fear and doing it anyway'. Not feeling the fear and doing it anyway but 'understanding it' first!

You don't have a syndrome! In the majority of cases you do not need to pathologise this and believe you are abnormal.

It's critical for you to realise *impostor syndrome* is not a medical condition (as I said, it's not recognised in the 2 main classifications). You do not have a deficiency which is part of your personal identity. You have a challenge which is part of the human condition, although it can be more extreme for certain people than others.

Be open to the belief you are not an impostor, but just grappling with challenges every human being faces from time to time. If you hold onto the position that you are an impostor, you will likely seek out evidence to support this as part of your need to confirm this view. Your *ego* can be playing out here with its need to be right (see more in the *ego* chapter).

During workshops with business leaders in the past, I've done a poll at the beginning and asked how many people believed they had *impostor syndrome* (along with the other 4 areas of the *survival psychology* model). There are invariably people who put themselves in this camp at the start, but on many occasions at the end the number in the *impostor syndrome* camp goes to zero, having understood all of the 5 areas more clearly.

Know you are good enough. Not being good enough is your underlying fear driven by your *survival psychology*. You are not perfect and never will be. You want to continue to grow and develop on your leadership journey and never become complacent. But don't do this from a place of continually believing you are not good enough.

Do things to boost your mood and mindset, many of which are covered in the later chapter on *negative self-talk*.

<u>Important point</u>

If after reading all of this chapter, your feelings of being an impostor still feel too strong and debilitating, it is worth seeking 121 coaching, therapy or medical support.

* Practical tools and actions for you

Here are a number of practical tools and actions which will support you in the area of *impostor syndrome*. Select the 1 or 2 you feel addresses your biggest challenges and focus on these first.

a) Shift your mindset from a place of consciousness

At all times we should be aware we can use the power only known to be gifted to our species - the ability to be consciously aware of and rise above our own thoughts. From this vantage point we can make choices. We can leave ourselves on auto pilot and follow the well-worn path laid out by the belief we have *impostor syndrome* with all the negative thoughts associated with this. Alternatively, we can consciously choose a different path to follow and firm up. One where we understand it, see it as normal and see it impacts everyone. We can choose to think about and see ourselves differently and in a much more positive way. We can be kinder and more compassionate with ourselves, rather than being hijacked by self-criticism and doubt.

As part of this, we must move from an inner monologue, where we far too often accept the 1,000s of thoughts we have every day as the truth. We need to move to an inner dialogue, where the 'potential self' within us challenges the 'destructive self' (and its drive to make us believe we are an impostor). The greater ability you have to disassociate from your imposter voice (and in conjunction with this the voice of your fears) by having rational conversations with it, the more you can weaken its hold.

b) Work on your 'Success, Strengths and Skills Script'

Within this, you examine and capture all your successes and achievements from when you were born through to today. Not just at work and not just the big ones. Capture all your achievements over time.

Then look at the strengths you were either genetically born with or those strengths which have become part of your character over time. It could be you are very well organised or you're a great communicator. Doing this is an excellent opportunity to focus on the all the strengths you possess and not the strengths you don't have.

For your skills, look at the areas you've been trained in, your academic achievements, your training qualifications, your professional certifications, as well as other areas (such as more informal training and on the job coaching). It's all part of the brilliant you!

Go deeper and remember what contributed to all 3 of these areas and how it made you feel at the time or how it makes you feel now.

Not only will doing this be a positive experience, in terms of validating and reinforcing the person you are, but I recommend using this as a resource going forwards. In different scenarios you can read through this to bolster your emotional and psychological state.

It might be you're giving a big presentation, you could be going to an important meeting, maybe you have a significant sales opportunity. Regardless, it's a useful tool or reference piece to go back to and refresh your memory to help put you in a positive state in the situation you are about to go into.

I gave a female leader this exercise and she came back from it saying she didn't realise how much she had achieved and how much she had developed. It gave her the confidence to go for a more senior role in another company.

Additionally, I recommend you write your life story down, capturing the high and the low points. Appreciate the many challenges you've come through on the journey of life for you, and where you've got to today.

c) Use a technique called the 'Circle of Excellence'

The 'Circle of Excellence' (a self-anchoring process originally developed by Dr. John Grinder, the co-creator of NLP) is a technique where you visualise and step into your own 'Circle of Excellence' to remember some of the amazing accomplishments and experiences of your life and fully connect with them to bring back the great feelings. Times when you felt confident, powerful, achieved a great result, felt loved. The experience of remembering all these past events vividly in your 'Circle of Excellence' will shift your emotional and psychological state. As with your Succes, Skills & Strengths Script, you can then use this to shift your state as you prepare or go into an important meeting, presentation or speech.

d) Utilise evidence to challenge your impostor syndrome beliefs

Continually challenge yourself, as if in a court of law, with irrefutable evidence of your progress and achievements (your script and circle of excellence above can form part of this). Challenge your belief that you are an impostor, as if you were supporting a close friend or colleague impacted by this. Be alert to when it is taking hold and make a conscious choice to shift your perspective to a more empowering one. With time, the new belief will begin to become more firmly wired in your brain and will feel a more automatic choice.

e) Seek honest feedback from others and believe the good

We will cover the area of feedback in much more detail in the *defensive mindset* chapter but be receptive to any positive feedback which will challenge your impostor feelings. You may need to process any critical feedback constructively but believe the good and ask for more specific detail when you receive this as it will reinforce its validity.

Use this to support the view that your successes are yours to own. They are not down to luck, a fluke, someone else (you can acknowledge others' roles in them) or invalid positive views of others.

f) Don't chase external validation

Look less for external validation, in the form of more qualification. When one of my clients tells me they are going to take a new qualification I ask, why? If they are taking the path due to an interest or it having utility in relation to a goal or outcome, then this is fair enough. Often though, I sense the path to more qualifications can be down to feelings of being an impostor. Leaders can feel the need to wear qualifications like a badge of proof they are worthy of their position and title. Many of the most successful business people across the planet have no recognised qualifications. If it's truly holding you back, go for it. If it is your mindset holding you back, deal with that!

g) Accept yourself as unique

I carried out a fascinating interview with Caroline Flanagan (episode 54), on my podcast series 'Leadership Mindset' in 2023. Caroline is an *impostor syndrome* coach for lawyers. She does a lot of work with lawyers on the challenges faced by the experience of feeling an impostor. Caroline's mission is also to increase diversity and inclusion in law by supporting minority individuals to know their value, contribute more of who they are, and fulfil their true potential - which I think is a fantastic mission. It also recognises that the feeling of being an impostor can impact on different groups of society in different ways.

In the interview, Caroline shared her background and experiences as a black woman. She spoke about the unique journey she's experienced throughout her life, when she's been in school or other circumstances, where she might have been the only black woman. Situations like this could initially have led her to feel uncomfortable, feel isolated or fraudulent. But through time, she's learned to accept these feelings as part of her own unique journey. It's part of the normalisation which is important for us all.

We all need to realise we don't need to continually look over our shoulder and compare to other people as our benchmark. We need to focus and understand that we've had our own unique path which has taken us to where we are. We all have our own valuable experiences we bring to the table. The fact we are different doesn't in any way make us a fraud. There should be more of an acceptance of who you are and your own uniqueness.

h) Create a development plan for your new position

A new position or promotion in work can cause issues relating to *impostor syndrome*. Rather than harbour doubts about the gaps in your skills or feel embarrassed about what you feel you should know, be open with your senior leader about your gaps in knowledge and skills. Nobody should be expecting you to walk into a position as the complete article, you are there very much based on your potential. People need to be supported through moves to new positions. If your employer expects you to pick everything up day one, that is a red flag and needs a serious conversation.

Talk to key people about where the gaps lie. Have an open conversation about those areas you perceive you might have a need to improve and how they feel you can increase your strengths and skills in those areas. You can then develop a plan to close them over time, working with the support of others (including external support). Don't isolate yourself, don't keep this to yourself, talk to other people about it.

i) It's never too late to develop your skills as a head of an organisation

If you find yourself heading up an organisation and you have never had any leadership development, consider working with others who can support and develop you. If you feel you are genuinely equipped to lead and grow yourself without this, I respect your view.

I've met and worked with a number of organisational heads over the years, who have reached a point where they've questioned their ability to take things further alone (it may have been triggered by imposterism, but it can also be a valid analysis). Training, a Director's programme, 121 work with a coach, mentor or leadership psychologist could well bring a development in skills, confidence and personal growth. You are not an impostor. You are making a mature decision to grow as a leader with the support of others.

j) Move out of your comfort zone in managed steps

When you make moves which take you out of your comfort zone, it's worth doing this in managed steps, if this is feasible. Don't put yourself through extreme change unnecessarily as this will be more likely to trigger feelings of self-doubt or being an impostor.

When you step out and make mistakes, know this is completely normal. We will explore the area of making mistakes in more detail in the *defensive mindset* chapter but know making mistakes does not imply you are a failure. Nothing great has been achieved without them!

k) Keep a lid on the perfectionism

This will be covered elsewhere, but it directly relates to impostor feelings. We strive for perfection to prove ourselves. This can put you under extreme pressure, as the need to be seen as perfect can permeate through everything you do. Be clear on the areas which really need the highest of standards and work to improve those, but perfectionism will lead to overworking and all the issues with stress and feeling overwhelmed which come with this. The costs of perfectionism for you are very high.

Nothing in life or work is perfect. This is an illusion your impostor voice doesn't grasp. It's highly likely striving for perfection to prove yourself will be a never-ending journey, so work on the underlying problem which is really going on.

I) 'Act As If' you are confident

It's important to build your confidence as a leader. The biggest tragedy for people believing they have *impostor syndrome* and being impacted by the feeling of not good enough is it drains confidence.

A technique to bolster confidence is to 'Act As If' you're confident in various situations, such as giving presentations or holding important meetings. The technique comes from the work of psychologist William James in the early 1900's, where he spoke about 'Acting As If' you are confident. When you behave in this way your body language starts to influence your psychology. This is not faking it, but instead reinforcing your psychology by using more confident body language. It's ok to step forwards with heightened confidence into new situations as this will elevate your mindset, as long as this doesn't become delusional.

m) Get out there to share your knowledge and views

Whether it be as a thought leader, speaker or author you have your own unique take on topics. Your inner voice will scream you will be found out to be a fraud or unworthy, but the more you grow and learn the more you should share your experiences and knowledge.

I'm currently working with a Director who has 2 key objectives from his CEO - firstly to write his first book and secondly to speak on his areas of expertise at industry events. He has a wealth of experience and expertise to share with the world and this will be a brilliant journey for him.

I'm not an expert on *impostor syndrome.* I have practical experience, theoretical knowledge and personal opinions on how it plays out for people and how they can do something about the challenges. I want to share this to help other leaders.

If I'd listened to my inner voice too much, this book would not be in existence.

n) Be mindful of your language and how you speak to yourself

We'll be covering this in more detail in the chapter on *negative self-talk.*

You may want to develop some positive or reassuring affirmations for certain situations. I have something I say on a regular basis to myself when I'm going to see a new client or a big client or deliver important presentation.

And this is what I say: "I will do my best today. I will show up with a good heart, the wisdom I have developed through experience, integrity, professionalism, a growth mindset and my emotional intelligence to serve and make a difference."

o) Celebrate the good

Capture at least 5 good things about each day (as described in other areas of this book) as it will rewire your neural network and how you see yourself.

Celebrate and reward yourself for significant achievements and remember to keep adding to your Success, Strengths & Skills Script too.

Celebrate the achievements of others in your team too, as they are no doubt having their own inner battles with feeling an impostor.

p) Take regular time out to reflect

This is a repeated theme in this book. Take time to reflect on the good (and you can then capture and update things like your Success, Skills & Strengths Script) and the things which have not gone so well. Do this from a place of learning and growth, without your impostor voice hijacking you.

Regular time out (every 3 months) with a coffee and some quiet will enable you to take hold of life's lessons from a place of calm. Reflect on the good things and challenges from the past 3 months. Take an honest stock of your current strengths and weaknesses. How can you use your strengths to greater effect and what can you do to bolster your areas of weakness?

q) Be the light for others

I leave you with one final important action. We know everybody experiences moments when they feel 'not good enough' or like an impostor. The more we can be open about our own experiences, however uncomfortable they may seem, the more others will realise they are not on their own.

This will allow you to seek support and also offer it too. The more you see it in others and help them, the more aware and in control of it you become yourself. It's a big secret we shouldn't be perpetuating. We can beat this even more effectively together.

Summary

- First of all, you do not have a syndrome. It's not a clinical issue for the majority of people. We all have moments where we don't feel good enough, we all have moments where we feel we may be found out. It's part of the human condition and our survival thinking. We should talk about it more openly between ourselves and realise it's part of our evolution

- There are a number of challenges leaders face on a day-to-day basis, often through the belief they have *impostor syndrome*. Examples include - avoiding going for promotions, procrastination, paralysis, self-sabotage, perfectionism, expertism, people pleasing, self-deprecation, and guilt about success. In the worst cases, this can lead to mental health conditions such as stress, depression and anxiety

- Through a better understanding of what's going on you will gain a greater hold and power over this belief. This will be supported by using the tools I've been referencing and by being consciously aware of your own thinking, monitoring it, and knowing you can choose a different path.

Now let's examine how we can go into our defensive bubble to protect ourselves from the threats posed by making mistakes, receiving critical feedback and facing challenges which will take us out of our comfort zone and may well require us to develop our skills further.

2. DEFENSIVE MINDSET

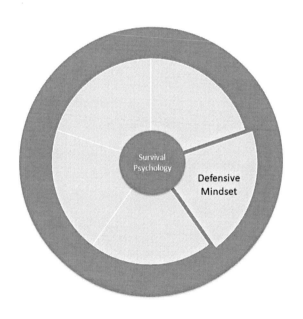

"You go into your protective bubble to keep yourself safe, but getting out of it provides the opportunities to truly grow."

Mindset is how we view our world

Mindset relates to how you see the world and your worldview. It's your set of beliefs about yourself, other people, your organisation and the wider world. Your worldview will very much determine whether your experiences are ones of happiness, success and growth or they are governed by anxiety, fear and defence.

A big part of my work with leaders is enabling them to shift their thinking so they can see their world differently and do more of the right things. Far too many Leaders have their heads down focusing on the endless list of tasks and the things they need to do. Finding some space to stand back and shift their thinking means they can change how they see themselves, see other people and see their organisation and will enable them to do the right things from a place of consciousness.

Your mindset will be determined by your thinking. Your path and the results you achieve will be directly impacted and changed by your thoughts and perspectives. This is why mindset is an important concept and understanding how you can go into a *defensive mindset* will aid your journey of growth and success.

Our defensive bubble

When we feel threatened our *survival psychology* will naturally want to put us into defensive mode, both physiologically and psychologically. It wants to keep us safe, but it can often be counterproductive for us. We can spend too much time in a defensive bubble. Going defensive is designed to keep us safe and is fear based, because exposing ourselves to things outside of the defensive bubble will feel threatening. This directly relates to the previous chapter on *impostor syndrome*, where I spoke about moving out of comfort zones and feeling threatened because of the fear of being found to be a fraud. Within this chapter, we are looking at the defensive bubble and the defensive position we can all get into when we are impacted by challenges, mistakes, failures or the need to change and do new things.

You may well be too young for this, but in 1976 I watched a film called 'The Boy in the Plastic Bubble', featuring John Travolta. It was based on true stories of people with a critical condition where it could be life threatening to be exposed to unfiltered air. In the film, John Travolta had to stay in a protective enclosure in his home and he could only attend college by wearing something like a spacesuit.

Many of us do this on a daily basis (metaphorically speaking!). We put ourselves in a defensive bubble. We protect ourselves from challenges, mistakes, failures, threats, but the problem with going defensive is it limits our potential to grow, especially in leadership roles. We need to make moves out of our 'protective bubbles' because, for us, it's typically not a matter of life and death as it was for John Travolta's character. Part of the problem is our *survival psychology* may well mistakenly judge it to be that way.

The path of growth

Rather than going defensive in the face of challenges, mistakes and such like, we always have the option to choose a path of growth. We can remain aware that we'll never be perfect or the finished article, but we can constantly learn and grow. Awareness is a key antidote to going into a *defensive mindset* and will be a consistent theme throughout this chapter.

Richard Branson, Bruce Springsteen, Michael Jordan and other high achievers in the worlds of business, arts and sport did not get there by continually going into a *defensive mindset*. All have acknowledged making mistakes and getting things wrong on their journey. It has been their path of growth.

An understanding of the fear-based triggering which can trip us all up will aid the path of growth, rather than defence. The earlier part of this chapter is designed to do this for you. Awareness will give you power.

Triggers which create defensiveness

Unfortunately, there are several triggers which can put us into a *defensive mindset* or a defensive position.

- It may well be a block in the road or a challenge on the path to completing a task or project
- It could be a mistake or failure
- It could be feedback from somebody which is more critical in nature or even a customer complaint (especially if you're in a more front facing role)
- It could be the impact of change and the need for new skills required in relation to this
- It could be the need to make an important decision which carries with it some risks

All these kinds of triggers can take us into a defensive position.

Handling threats is a critical part of our *survival psychology*. Our survival thinking will want to keep us safe. It will want to put us in a protective bubble when exposed to any of these triggers. The more we can recognise when we've moved into a more defensive position and shift ourselves into what is termed a growth mindset (made famous by renowned psychologist Carole Dweck) the greater opportunity we will have to fulfil our potential.

Going into a *defensive mindset* is linked to the challenge of 'not feeling good enough' which is unfortunately a part of the human condition. Mistakes, failures, feedback and challenges can all threaten our self-esteem and our self-worth. They can often reinforce a position where we feel we're 'not good enough' in both our professional life and our personal life.

Our need to prove ourselves

Delving into the concept of *ego* for a moment (more coming in the next chapter), we are gripped by the need to prove ourselves. Often when we get defensive, it's because we are protecting *ego*. The need to deflect, blame, criticise and judge others will be very much based on *ego*. It's part of a range of defence mechanisms we will come to shortly.

Ego can hinder your growth as a leader, as can your *defensive mindset*. However, growth is at the very heart of what it means to be human, or to be any living entity.

Growth is a part of everyday language

It's worth noting there are many commonly used quotes in life which demonstrate the concept of having a growth mindset. It's part of us appreciating things aren't necessarily going to be easy on the path of growth.

- "Nothing ventured, nothing gained"

- "Rome wasn't built in a day"
- "Where there's a will there's a way"

Language is powerful and it's often a representation of the journey of life.

The defensive to growth spectrum

We all exist on a spectrum from defence to growth. We can go defensive in certain scenarios, or we go into a growth mindset in others. It's never black and white and we will never be permanently in a growth mindset or *defensive mindset*. Certain events, situations and people can trigger us to move into one of those mindsets more than other scenarios. We do however have the ability to consciously choose our position.

Whether traits and mindset positions are more permanent or variable links to the work of Cognitive Neuroscience where 'incremental theorists' believe traits are malleable as opposed to the views of 'entity theorists' who see traits as fixed. Socio Cognitive Personality Theory also supports the view that personalities are fluid and will change over time. The schools of thought which see personality traits as more malleable and fluid are in keeping with the view we have the potential to continually grow and develop our skills and abilities. This is a very positive view of human beings which is developed further by the concept 'neuroplasticity'.

Neuroplasticity – Scientific proof of our ability to change and grow

If you haven't come across the term 'neuroplasticity' before, it could be one of the greatest words to enter your vocabulary!

It was believed, more than 30 years ago, a person's development was pretty much finished in their early years. But through neuroscience, we have found the brain can be rewired and change shape right the way through to old age. It's what is termed neuroplasticity. It's the foundation for realising we have much greater potential to grow throughout our lives than we might have once believed. We can continually re-wire and re-programme ourselves.

Our ability to do this ties back again to the views of Cognitive Neuroscience, Socio Cognitive Personality Theory and Carole Dweck, seeing human beings as more fluid and able to grow and develop over time.

Robert Sternberg, a present-day guru on intelligence, proposes the major factor in whether people achieve expertise isn't down to fixed personality traits, but purposeful engagement. Through engagement and repeated behaviour, we can continue to wire and rewire our brain.

There's an amazing piece of research which was carried out with London taxi drivers (by Ella Maguire of U.C.L.). To earn their licenses and pass the test (known as 'The Knowledge'), taxi drivers in training spend 3 to 4 years driving around the city on mopeds, memorising a network of 25,000 streets within a 10-kilometer radius of Charing Cross train station, as well as thousands of tourist attractions.

Maguire followed a group of 79 aspiring taxi drivers for 4 years to measure the growth of their hippocampus (a complex brain structure embedded deep into temporal lobe which has a major role in learning and memory) with magnetic resonance imaging (MRI) as they completed The Knowledge. She also measured brain growth in 31 similar people who did not drive taxis. At the start of the study, all the participants had more or less the same size hippocampi. 4 years later 39 of the 79 trainees had earned their licenses and MRIs showed the successful trainees' hippocampi had grown over time.

If you've been around London, you'll know the road network is much more complicated than many other major cities, particularly if you look at cities in America like New York, for example. By exercising this part of their brain every day, London taxi drivers actually changed the shape of their brain and their neurons.

Recognising the ability to change the brain is an incredibly optimistic view of the human species and it's an optimistic view I want you to take away for yourself. You can exercise and develop your neural network and your brain. The brain can continue to form new connections and change shape when we learn new things. Continual work can be done to build our long-term memory to source from in the future.

Brainwaves tell a story

Carole Dweck carried out a piece of research in her lab in Columbia where she examined the brain-waves of people with different mindsets, growth and fixed (in her terms). People with a more fixed mindset, who believed there skills were fixed, were only interested in feedback when it related to their ability. People with a growth mindset paid attention to information they could learn from to develop their skills and knowledge. Your mindset will determine how much you can change and rewire your brain.

The role of genes and heritability

Gilbert Gottlieb, who's an eminent neuroscientist, states that not only do genes and the environment cooperate as we develop, but genes require input from the environment to work properly. We aren't victims of our genes; we are able to change and develop by the experiences we face. We have much more control and power over our growth than we might believe. Knowing this will be a fuel for growth and enable us to move more effectively out of defensive positions.

Even Alfred Binet, the inventor of the IQ test, believed education and practice will bring about fundamental changes in intelligence. He therefore did not see intelligence as fixed.

The above all supports us in seeing our potential to continually grow, rather than believing our abilities, intelligence and skills are static. It can take us out of defensive positions, triggered by our survival thinking.

I have seen many leaders over the years develop new skills and expertise – become more strategic, creative, improve public speaking skills (significantly!), develop new technical skills. Stop telling yourself you can't change and be open to the fact that you can change, step by step.

Emotional intelligence

The ability to choose a path of growth also relates to your emotional intelligence. There are 5 aspects to *emotional intelligence* (in Daniel Goleman's model) and the first 3 relate to self:

- Self-awareness
- Self-management
- Self-motivation
  (the other 2 are empathy and relationship management).

All 3 of these will impact on whether you go into a defensive bubble or not. It's accepted people can improve their emotional intelligence in all 5 areas and specifically the 3 relating to self, which support our potential to grow in what could otherwise be seen to be threating or negative situations.

Empathy and relationship management are the areas of Emotional Intelligence which will improve how you manage the *defensive mindset* of others.

Seeing a defensive mindset in others

It's helpful to recognise the *defensive mindset* in others, whether as a leader, parent, family member or friend. You can become more tuned to see a *defensive mindset* occurring in the people around you. Often becoming defensive is an automatic unconscious behaviour. Once we make ourselves more aware of this and we make other people more aware of it happening for them, we are more likely to be able to do something about it for ourselves and to help others.

Defensive mindset and relationships

Observing a *defensive mindset* in ourselves and others will impact on the quality of our relationships. Going defensive can affect relationships, both personal and professional. If mistakes are not owned, it can damage our relationships with others, especially if we are in a leadership position. It can be harmful for the wider culture too. If feedback is delivered in the wrong way to people in your teams, it can trigger a defensive position and people will take it personally without being receptive to the lessons therein. On the flip side, as leaders we need to be ready to take feedback from others, as it will build a relationship of trust.

Putting others in a defensive place or assuming this place ourselves can lead to a shutdown or conflict. It can destablise relationships, even stronger ones. If you're part of a culture which doesn't own mistakes, blames others, is unreceptive to feedback and doesn't push through challenges, it will be a culture built on fragile foundations with unsupportive relationships.

Be mindful that the use of language can impact whether people go into a defensive stance or not. Too much accusatory 'you' language can definitely do this, or language which is emotionally charged or overly harsh.

I've worked with senior leaders to help them re-word emails and adapt their style, as words in emails or messages can be quicky interpreted in a negative way and put people on the backfoot if worded. Often it's about thinking how you words will land and adapting them.

Defence mechanisms

There are many defensive behaviours used in the interest of allegedly protecting self. Psychologists Sigmund Freud and his daughter Anna Freud identified and studied a range of defence mechanisms.

Here are some examples of both theirs and other defence mechanisms:

Projection	We project the issues or weaknesses we have within ourselves onto other people.
Gaslighting	A variant of the above where lying and manipulation will be used to make someone else feel in the wrong.
Denial	Rather than face up to a reality which makes us uncomfortable, we block this from our conscious mind.
Altruism	Interestingly this can also be seen as a defence mechanism, where we look to fulfil the needs of others as a way of avoiding conflict.
Avoidance	Avoiding people or situations which may be challenging or emotionally

	triggering is a classic way to protect self and go into a *defensive mindset*.
Passive-Aggressive	We go into this state, rather than maturely dealing with a problem, by becoming stubborn, childish or sarcastic.
Aggression	Outright aggression is often a form of defence.
Lying	Rather than be found out for a mistake or something we've done wrong, we will tell a range of lies.
Humour	And finally our tendency to use humour or crack a joke to take the heat out of a difficult situation or avoid dealing with it. Often sarcasm and humour are used when a person feels vulnerable and they want to defend self.

These are examples of some of the defence mechanisms we use when we feel threatened, or our safety is at risk. Only by recognising we are using one of the mechanisms can we make conscious choices to move out of these states. Our ability to do this may well depend on how psychologically safe we feel in the environment we are in too.

Putting people into boxes due to labelling or stereotyping

We need to be very mindful of the labelling and stereotyping which can happen in life. Labelling someone will put them into a box, and it will give them a constrained view of their own potential.

People of colour know about being wrongly stereotyped with being lower in intelligence. Women know about being stereotyped as inferior in maths and science subjects. Research by Steele and Aronson showed even ticking a box to indicate race or sex can trigger stereotypes in people's minds and lower test scores. Labelling will constrain people's views of their potential and impact on a person's ability to grow. The views of society can impose restrictive views on our potential. It can take us out of a growth mindset and put us in boxes (the area of prejudice will be explored further in the *group behaviour* chapter). It's important we don't let the views of others influence our own views of our potential in damaging ways. It's a responsibility of wider society not to do this to others too.

CEO disease

The concept called 'CEO Disease' is where leaders at the top of the hierarchy don't confront their own shortcomings. It's often a disease which accompanies low emotional intelligence and high *ego*. CEOs with this are influenced by underlying insecurity and will surround themselves with people who will say "Yes" often removing any critics. It's a power-based demonstration of going into a *defensive mindset*. It will take CEOs to a place where they are non-learners and it can restrict a growth culture more broadly. It will make them unreceptive to change, making them more controlling and even abusive and it can create a collective culture of fear and defensiveness.

Leaders with 'CEO Disease' need to take an honest appraisal of themselves and ideally work with a coach or psychologist to shift their mindset and behaviour. It may need courageous others to point this out for them too!

A culture of lying

CEO disease and other negative leadership traits can create a culture of fear and deceit from the top down. Scandal gripped the American energy company Enron in 2001 ending in bankruptcy. A culture of lying had influenced many within the organisation to cover up mistakes, internally fabricating financial records and falsifying the success of the company (you will see more about conformity and obedience in the *group behaviour* chapter). Lying became a collective 'defence mechanism'. As an example, a critical board meeting at

Enron in 1991 led to them giving approval to set aside their ethics statements to allow for inappropriate behaviour in relation to partnerships.

Not only can there be problems with the heads of companies, but as we see here, a culture of defensiveness can move right the way through an organisation. The *defensive mindset* engendered from the top had devastating consequences in 2001. Rather than face up to the things which have been done wrong, lies and deceit played out from a defensive position.

Growth needs realistic self-assessment

As I touched on in the chapter on *impostor syndrome* (and will do further in the chapter on *ego*) we need to be more honest in the assessment of our own capability. We need to healthily bolster our self-esteem by acknowledging our strengths and skills. We also need to be honest about our deficiencies and the areas which need work.

A *defensive mindset* can put us into more unrealistic territories when analysing our own capability. We may feel the need to delude ourselves from a place of defence, which can result in poor behaviour and lack of clarity on our path of growth.

My work with leaders always starts with my 'Leadership Diagnostic'. Within this there are a range of quantitative questions to examine personality, behaviour, emotional intelligence and *survival psychology*. There are also a range of questions to honestly reflect on areas which aren't going so well in the role, bad habits, skills to develop and relationships to work on. Being honest with ourselves will enable a clearer path to develop.

Fearing failure and the brain

Fearing failure can block us. It can stifle creativity and innovation and it can cause deeper issues for us psychologically too.

The 'amygdala', at the heart of the emotional part of the brain (the limbic system), triggers the fear activity within our biological system and our fight/flight/freeze response. It's also associated with memory, fear conditioning and our learned responses. We can learn to be afraid of a stimulus or experience which can trigger an automatic response. At its worst, this can drive us to a state known as 'Learned Helplessness' (from renowned psychologist Martin Seligman), where we believe whatever we do will have no positive impact.

I recently collaborated with a senior leader who believed he couldn't make the necessary changes in his area of the organisation because he thought his hands were tied. But when we examined this, there were a number of small steps that could be taken to make advances and these steps made the fear of failure feel more manageable.

If we consciously look to recover from and move through failures, we can condition ourselves, step by step, to become more resilient and confident in the face of adversity. Doing this gives us a mindset shift in the way we look at failure, but it also leads to a biological shift in how our brain is wired. It's something to be conscious of as an individual, but as a leader it's important to be mindful of this for others and the broader culture of your organisation.

A need to win or even just survive can make us too defensive

Many sports supporters become frustrated with their teams when they employ more defensive tactics, as it can be very unentertaining. Although the defensive behaviours can bear fruit in terms of results, the broader need to entertain paying supporters can be lost.

Going into a defensive position, as with *ego*, can be symptomatic of an all encompassing need to win. The need to win at all costs and often speedily, rather than taking a journey of longer-term persistent growth can be counterproductive. Don't let an obsession with winning and a need for quick wins divert you from a path of sustainable long-term growth and your true purpose.

It's important to acknowledge that it's not always about winning. Often, we can go defensive because we are in a genuinely threatening situation for our survival. Survival can be a real and need serious action to return us to a safe and secure place. It's still important to avoid going too defensive in these scenarios, as getting on the front foot will be key to your survival.

Having the patience to grow and be creative

Often growth is achieved through patience and spending time on tasks. Once we go defensive it will block our steady growth. It will hijack us and demonstrate the range of more negative and unproductive states and behaviours that we have been examining. Many of you will know the story of Thomas Edison and his 1,000 failed attempts to finally create a working light bulb (which is helping me write this book during the winter months).

A growth mindset will enable us to be more creative too. Going defensive will block our creativity, as creativity needs us to try things and fail or make mistakes. It's also known scientifically that creativity comes from a place where our brain operates at a low frequency. Slowing down is supported by behaviours which put the brain into a state where the frequency is 8 to 12 Hz (alpha waves), rather than in the more normal alert state of 12 to 25 Hz. Our *survival psychology* taking hold will make us more fearful or defensive, in turn raising our blood pressure and brain frequency and hindering our ability to be creative. Therefore, finding space and quiet to slow the brain down will release more of our creative powers.

In a poll of 143 creativity researchers (carried out by Richard Sternberg) there was wide agreement about the number one ingredient in creative achievement - it's exactly the kind of perseverance and resilience I've been talking about in relation to focusing on growth rather than defence.

Growth or defence – It's your conscious choice

As described earlier, we're never going to be 100% in a mindset of growth, although we should strive to move out of defence and into growth as much as possible. Sometimes we may get triggered into a *defensive mindset* and it can happen unconsciously. Once you recognise it, raise your awareness and take the steps to move out of it as quickly as possible. Be mindful of never letting this become part of your identity. Don't feel being defensive is a character trait or let failures and mistakes define you. Mindsets are part of your personality, but you can continually change them.

Let's examine a range of practical challenges which can result from being more defensive.

The mind-traps leaders face with defensive mindset

I've heard many direct examples of *defensive mindset* playing out for leaders through time:

- Giving up when pushed out of comfort zones or into the unknown
- Deliberating and procrastinating too much, especially when it involves money
- Overcooking consequences of things going wrong
- Being put on the backfoot too quickly when things go wrong
- Sticking to habits you know deep down are unhelpful
- Taking feedback personally and dismissing it
- Unable to be open and honest
- Seeing skills as fixed

Leaders can be uncomfortable sharing these kinds of thoughts with others in the organisation. It feels more comfortable doing this in a 121 session with me or during a confidential call. The problem is holding back keeps leaders and others inside the protective bubble and holds back their growth. I'm sure you may well relate to one or more of the real life examples above?

Let's explore a range of challenges which can hinder a leader's progress by being stuck in a *defensive mindset*.

Road blocks

First of all, a *defensive mindset* can be moved into when we experience blockers on projects or tasks. We've had ideas on a new direction, but it takes work. We will hit points where there are challenges or we reach perceived blocks on the path.

When we go into a more defensive place, we can get overwhelmed and can be inclined to give up or shut down. Our *survival psychology* may well feel this is the best route to keep us safe or protect our self-esteem. We can feel threatened, we retreat and we don't put in the necessary effort due to the need to keep ourselves safe or our self-image safe. All this denies us the chance to push through to find solutions and grow.

Mistakes and failure

The second challenge faced by leaders is when mistakes are made or failures are encountered. It's a tragedy, as we get older, we can lose the ability to keep pushing through when we experience mistakes and failure.

Thinking back to when we were babies and we started to walk, we would continually fall over. But we would pick ourselves up and go again. This ability to 'fail forwards' sadly diminishes as we go into adult life, if we allow our survival thinking to take hold of the steering wheel. Failing forwards is a term which describes how by failing, we actually demonstrate and realise we're making progress.

It's a fact of life that our goals and our journey will naturally bring about failures or mistakes. Our response will be determined by our mindset and our worldview. How will we view failure? By pushing through and finding solutions we can find a way forward and this will be a key part of our growth. This is the 'failing forwards' mindset we had as a baby.

Mistakes or failures can unfortunately make us defensive quite quickly. If somebody else talks to us about a mistake made, we might try to find every other reason rather than accept responsibility ourselves for the mistake (a blame culture in organisations will make this considerably worse!).

We all make mistakes. We're all human. I've worked on this myself over the years, to get myself in a place where I can accept I've made a mistake so I can learn and grow from it. In 1993 I made the biggest mistake of my career. I was responsible for database administration for the new council tax system at a local authority. I made a mistake that deleted all the accounts data without a proper back up and feared I would be sacked! But I worked with others to get this back and learnt the value of collaboration in resolving problems! I also learnt a number of lessons about how to do my work in the future to ensure nothing like this would happen again.

Allow yourself to accept you will make mistakes and learn from them. Remember to allow others to do the same.

How do you receive and give feedback?

How do you feel when someone offers you feedback? Do you welcome it as something you may learn from? Or do you want to go into a shell and ignore it? (Hint – the best response is the first one.)

When we are given more critical feedback, we can take it personally and it can bring out the feeling of 'not being good enough' as I've been describing throughout this book. It's at these times we've been hooked by our *survival psychology* trying to protect us. Becoming stronger and seeing feedback as valuable and something you can grow and build from will be important, especially if you're in a leadership role.

We always have the choice we don't need to take feedback on board if we don't believe it's valid. It's only one person's view after all, unless you source feedback from multiple sources and observe trends. On this note, 360-degree feedback is highly recommended for leaders. With this feedback, you source feedback on your performance from the people you lead, people at your level and more senior people.

If you're in an organisation where you're on the frontline and may receive customer complaints directly, do your best to listen and take them on board. See if you can do anything to resolve them and change the way you and others behave for the future.

If you're in a leadership position, giving feedback should be a regular feature of your behaviour. Be mindful the balance of positive to negative feedback should be at least 3:1 to improve performance (known as 'The Losada Line' based on the work of psychologist Marical Losada. He studied 60 organisations and found this ratio and higher was where teams performance was enhanced). Positive feedback will be a reinforcer of good behaviour and growth. When this is balanced with the ratio level of 3:1, positive to negative, it's less likely that more critical feedback will put people into a *defensive mindset* and how you deliver feedback will impact on this too. More of this shortly. We don't want to delude people. Ensure people are given feedback when things go wrong too but frame it in a way which is more likely to trigger a growth position rather than a defensive position.

Being drawn to the negative

It's also important to be mindful of how people receive positive feedback. Often, this will be rejected or dismissed too quickly. People's underlying sense of 'not being good enough' may well mean they won't take positive feedback as valid and are more likely to be drawn to any negative feedback.

When I was an Open University tutor, I would typically have a group of around 20 students. When I received the end of year feedback there would sometimes be 1 or 2 students who hadn't connected with me as well as the majority had. Rather than focus on the 18 or 19 students who seemed very happy with my role as a tutor, I would fixate on the 1 or 2 giving more negative feedback. Does this ring any bells reader?

My fixation stems from our general wiring to be more pessimistic in nature, rather than optimistic, as our survival radar firmly sets to pick out threats and danger. It was important for me to take the learnings from anything which was valid, in terms of more critical feedback, but I also needed to ensure I reinforced the good things I was doing and accept the positive. It's important for us all to do this in all aspects of our professional and private life.

We also need to help people in our teams keep a rational view on the feedback they receive. When you next give someone positive feedback and they dismiss it quickly, go into more detail about why what they did was important and in what ways it had a positive impact. Also, when people share good news with you, employ 'Active Conditional Responding' too. ACR is where you don't just say "well done", but you probe them on why this was important to them.

Moving out your comfort zone

The next challenge which can put leaders into a *defensive mindset* is where we get moved out of our comfort zone by having to learn something new or develop a new skill often because of internal or external changes. At the time of writing this book, 'Artificial Intelligence' is going through a massive surge in use, with tools coming out daily and the use of this expanding. We may perceive changes like this as threatening, causing us to either seek understanding or ignore them to protect ourselves. We can feel threatened by new developments and change, but only by getting out of our comfort zones will we be able to grow. Be mindful of not being triggered by the FOMO - Fear Of Missing Out - and make rationale choices on which changes need to be taken on board for you. Remember 'Clubhouse' anyone? This was an online networking and knowledge platform which rose speedily to prominence during the pandemic and everyone felt they needed to be on the platform, only for it to decline speedily too!

With regards to taking steps out of your comfort zone, it isn't about throwing yourself out of your comfort zone into extreme situations and what I would call the panic zone. It's about moving from a comfort zone and a place of defence into a growth zone to be able to change or adapt your skills. Discomfort in life is normal. It's part and parcel of the human condition and a sign you have the chance to grow. In modern life we have become too resistant to discomfort and many areas of discomfort get exaggerated and distorted to become a matter of survival (which in most cases they are not).

It may be, in order to do this, you need to work with somebody else and be coached, mentored or trained. It may be you need to do some reading or research. It may mean you have to do some practical on the job work experience. All of these will take you out of your comfort zone. But managed calmly, they will take you into a growth zone where you learn new things, grow and improve steadily. It's also worth being clear on the most suitable way to learn for you, as this can guide the best methods for you to acquire new skills. Are you more practical in the way you learn, or are you more academic in nature, for example?

The alternative to this is to retreat and go into our protective bubble and avoid changes and new things. It's been the undoing of many leaders and the death of companies, where they haven't embraced the changes which have come through. Polaroid, Blockbuster and Blackberry are all examples of failed companies who didn't respond well to change.

Being threatened by the success of others

The next defensive challenge is when we are threatened by other people's success and this links directly to the role of *ego*.

We don't focus on our own path of growth, but we get fixated on what somebody else is doing and how they may be doing it better. Yes, we can learn from other people (as I described in relation to moving out of comfort zones), but often it's much better to focus on our own race and our own path.

In 1981, John McEnroe bought a black Les Paul guitar and the same week he went to see Buddy Guy play in Chicago. Instead of seeing this as inspiration he went home and smashed his guitar to pieces. Very often we can all feel like metaphorically 'smashing our guitar' when we see someone who is more capable. We give in because we don't match up to someone else's level, but we don't see the work which has gone into reaching this level. We don't realise it's our journey, with our own unique goals and aims that has value itself.

Making decisions... or not

We often come to pivotal points on our journey. There have been some critical ones over the past few years for us all, particularly in relation to the pandemic that impacted the whole world. Often, the need to make bigger decisions in a position of leadership can put us back in the protective bubble of procrastination. Our *survival psychology* will leave us in a place of fear and in overwhelming situations one reaction is to 'freeze' and stay still. This form of deferment can be due to the potential physical or practical consequences of getting something wrong, but it can also be based on a fear of looking foolish or 'not good enough'.

We mostly indulge in procrastination to keep ourselves safe and secure. If we don't decide and stay where we are, we think we're not going to put ourselves in a difficult or risky situation. But making no decision is risky too! By making no decision and procrastinating there's a level of risk, as there would be in deciding and moving forwards. Procrastination directly relates to the defence mechanism of avoidance, which we covered earlier. We avoid making decisions because they feel threatening due to our *survival psychology* being triggered.

It is worth considering how often decisions can be made where the risks or impacts of things going wrong is not too significant. We can move forwards on a path and if things don't totally work out, we can alter the path. I had an interesting conversation with one of my daughter's friends several years ago, when she was talking about going on the path to become a nurse. She looked at me and said "What if it doesn't work out?" and I looked at her and said "You're 20 years old, you will just do something different".

We can make decisions feel much bigger than they are and can exaggerate the dangers of failure associated with them. But deciding to go on a path doesn't have to be fixed, we can change again. Often, we can move forwards and then check after time whether it still seems like the right decision. If it doesn't then alter the path. As a leader, you can do this collectively with your teams too.

If it's a big decision, we can also go through risk analysis. In my days as a project manager in an IT department, we would often carry out risk analysis. The millennium bug in software being a classic case of this. When we were to flip from 1999 to 2000 at midnight on December 31st, the world feared computer systems across the world would cause serious problems. We conducted an in-depth risk analysis for this project, with a multitude of actions planned to minimise risk and handle negative outcomes.

Trust your intuition more

It's also interesting to note we have a neurology in both our heart and in our stomach. People often link the intelligence residing in our gut to phrases like 'gut instinct'. Trust your intuition and your implicit knowledge more when you're deciding, as there's a whole wealth of experience living in your unconscious which you can have more faith in.

There is the famous story of the Chicago firefighter who, when handling what seemed a strange and uneasy situation at a house fire, ordered his team to "get out now!". Moments later the floor they had been standing on collapsed. He had observed the water was not putting out the fire, the living room was unusually hot, and the fire was unusually quiet. His intuition had recognised this pattern and he knew the situation was not safe, even though not fully conscious of what was going on in the moment.

Beliefs can be rooted deeply within us

Our beliefs about ourselves, about how mistakes are to be handled and about our world view may well have developed over a long period of time. Family, life experiences and events has influenced them in the world. We can metaphorically weaken the supporting legs under them, but they may show up in the future. Self-limiting beliefs will often put us in a more defensive place.

Challenging our beliefs is at the core of Cognitive Therapy, developed by Aaron Beck. Becoming more aware of our constraining or self-limiting beliefs allows us to look for evidence which challenges and weakens them. You can challenge the evidence supporting these unhelpful beliefs objectively. For example, is there a successful person on the planet who has never made a mistake?

Additionally, the more we can build new beliefs based on a view of growth, the more they can counter the older more defensive beliefs. As you strengthen these they will support and enable you more on the journey.

Having better internal dialogues, which will enable you to challenge unhelpful beliefs and build helpful ones, will be explored more in the chapter on *negative self-talk*.

The impact of defence mechanisms

The next challenge is around dealing with the many defensive mechanisms I spoke about earlier in this chapter - projection, gaslighting, denial, repression, avoidance, lying or even aggression.

All of these will ultimately cause difficulties, both in our relationships with other people and our relationship with self.

Be much more self-aware when you've been hijacked by one of these defensive mechanisms as it will provide you with greater power to get out of it.

Also know your red flags when other people using defence mechanisms. I spoke with an MD recently where he had become aware one of his team had been lying to him to cover up things that had not been done. It's important to note that this was not an oppressive culture that didn't tolerate mistakes and occasional missed tasks. Lying was a huge red flag for the MD and had negative consequences for the relationship.

Triggering defensive positions in others

Be very clear we can easily trigger a defensive position or a *defensive mindset* in other people. The way we handle our relationships and communicate with other people can either put people more into a growth mindset, where they are more likely to listen and engage positively, or it can put them in a defensive place, where they will feel threatened. Pushing people into a more self-justifying place can lead to all sorts of problems in relationships, right the way from a breakdown in the relationship through to acts of verbal or physical aggression.

Significant life experiences

Sometimes we can be incredibly unfortunate and impacted by big challenges in life. Christopher Reeve was thrown from a horse in 1995 leaving him paralysed. Against the views of doctors, he embarked on an exercise regime which led to him regaining movement in various parts of his body.

Serious life events can very much put us on the back foot, but we always have a choice as to how we will face them.

I've covered some ideas on meeting the challenges of being defensive, so now let me share what you can do, both with regards to mindset and practical actions.

How to escape the mind-traps of a defensive mindset

* Mindset

Conscious awareness of what is going on psychologically is key, as with all 5 aspects of the *survival psychology* model.

It's important to recognise that adopting a defensive mindset really aims to keep us safe. It puts us in a protective bubble, rather than exposing ourselves to the challenges of dealing with potential threats, mistakes, feedback or challenges we may be encountering. But the problem is it inhibits our growth and ultimately doesn't keep us safer in the long term.

We are human. We will make mistakes or fail at times. Other people will criticise us. It's part of the journey of life and needs to be embraced more in our worldview. A healthy place is to see ourselves as 'good enough' as a human being, but simultaneously know we can continually grow and improve in all aspects of life and work. I'm sorry to say to all the perfectionists out there, we are never the finished article and the things we do are never finished. We can continually improve, develop and grow and this is a good place to be for our mental health too.

It's also important we don't get on a path of bolstering the *ego* (as we will come to in more detail next chapter), but remain on a path of personal growth by acknowledging all the weaknesses, mistakes and areas we can work on in ourselves.

The path of growth is one in which we seek to get a little better each day and eventually we will end up in a place where we are a whole lot better.

* Practical tools and actions for you

Here are a number of practical tools and actions which will support you in relation to *defensive mindset*. Select the 1 or 2 you feel addresses your biggest challenges and focus on these first.

a) Be the role model

As a leader, how you handle mistakes, failure, feedback and challenges will be a guide for others. They won't follow what you say, they will follow how you behave. Use every opportunity to mindfully move yourself out of a *defensive mindset* and into a growth mindset as the model for your people.

Be prepared to own mistakes, take feedback and show some vulnerability when appropriate, as part of being a more authentic leader. If you're willing to reflect honestly and feel either your skills or behaviour need some support, don't hold back in looking for a psychologist, coach or trainer who can help you improve your mindset and skills as a leader.

When Jack Welch took over GE in 1980, the company was valued at $14B. In 2000 it was valued at $490B. Welch was renowned as someone who kept his *ego* in check and led with a growth mindset. 1,000 of hours were spent coaching and developing executives, rather than hiring based on existing pedigree. His language was also rooted in the use of "We" rather than "I" (a theme we will explore in the chapters on *ego* and *group behaviour*).

Start with a belief in human potential and be a catalyst for the growth mindsets in others (which I'll expand on when we get to growth culture)

b) Seek help from experts

If you identify areas where you need help with your mindset, look to work with a psychologist, coach or trainer. It could be in relation to emotional intelligence, defence mechanisms or other areas covered in the main text, where you realise you can't resolve them on your own.

The best leaders acknowledge their areas of development and work with others to improve them. You can do so much yourself, but your limitations and blind spots may well need the help and support of others.

c) The 3-step method to handle mistakes, feedback and challenges

You can use this 3-step method if a mistake has happened, you've had some negative feedback or your *defensive mindset* has been triggered in some way.

- First of all, become aware you've been triggered and distance yourself, so you can take a bird's-eye view of the situation.
- Then analyse the situation and reflect on any thoughts or learnings objectively.
- Finally move forward and take action.

The 3-step process will enable you to deal more healthily with mistakes, feedback and blockers.

I met professional footballer Lee Dixon in the 1993 on holiday in Jamaica and followed his career after that holiday right the way through to him being a TV pundit. He once said on TV, as part of the England team they learned way more from the defeats than they ever did from the victories. In reality, we can learn from both, but it's important whenever we get gripped in a defensive position, we take those 3 steps and get to a more productive place.

d) Stop, start, continue or improve

When you're reflecting on mistakes, failures, blockers or feedback, look at this in 4 ways.

- What must you stop doing as a result of this?
- What must you start doing?
- What will you continue to do?
- What will you improve?

Take the learnings and make changes.

e) Moving out of comfort zones

Notice when you're staying in your comfort zone, either in a specific situation or in a broader sense.

Identify what 1 or 2 small steps you can take to move yourself out of your comfort zone, which you know is hindering your growth, and create a plan to do this steadily.

If you need the support and guidance of others to do this, don't hesitate to work with other people.

f) Repeated intentional action will rewire your neurology

We know the power of neuroplasticity. Focused repetition will lead to rewiring and will ultimately change your world view and mindset. The way you repeatedly handle blockers, mistakes, failure, feedback and decision making will become more automatic the more you do it. If you approach this with the intent of moving speedily out of defensive positions and into a growth mindset it will start to become your default position over time.

g) Know and use you learning style

One size doesn't fit all and as I wrote earlier, we can all learn in different ways. The classic 'Honey and Mumford' assessment sees learning styles in 4 ways – Activist, Pragmatist, Theorist and Reflector. Know what suits you best and engage with new learning in the way which is best for you.

There is also the VARK model where we are seen to have a preference for engaging with material in different ways – Visual, Auditory, Read/Write and Kinaesthetic (where we physically work with something). Again, you will know what suits you best so you can then request or use information in the best way. For example, many people like audiobooks but for me I prefer to read a hard copy (and highlight interesting parts).

h) Regular reflection time and space

Put time in your diary, every month or quarter, to reflect on:

- What you have done well
- What has not gone well and can be improved
- What are the key learnings from the month
- What are the goals and priorities for the next month

If you're a leader, do this regularly with your people. Through this you will embed new habits and stop habits which are unproductive on your path of growth.

Quality time is also thinking space. It's time when you can slow down your brain frequency and enable you to think more creatively about strategy, projects and problems. It's also time for you to push yourself to make decisions without the cut and thrust of the daily activities. It's time to push yourself out of your defensive comfort zone, stop procrastinating and take bold steps forwards.

Regular reflection time is time to work on yourself too. What are the beliefs holding you and your team back? How can you challenge them and put in place more empowering beliefs? What defence mechanisms are you lapsing into and need addressing? As touched on earlier, it may be all these areas of reflection may be best supported by a psychologist or coach.

i) Working with the support of other people

When you hit a big challenge speak to other people. Don't let your *defensive mindset* (or *ego*) make you feel threatened by doing this. You may have hit a roadblock and you could talk to other people who have experienced this before and found a way through it. Don't let your *ego* get in the way here. If you're a senior leader, look at other people right across the organisation. You could bring in experts from outside the organisation too if needed.

Talk to people who've got more experience or are more expert, because they may well be able to help you move forwards speedily.

When I wanted to improve my keynote and do a TEDx talk, I started working with Helen Packham, who has been a TEDx event curator. This not only raised my game and got me a TEDx talk, but things moved more speedily with expert help.

j) Have courageous conversations

Silence (or going into a passive place) can be a form of defence. It means our views aren't expressed or heard and our valuable input can be lost. We fear upsetting people, looking stupid or challenging other people's views. The result is we retreat into ourselves and we don't value our own feelings and opinions enough. True growth needs us to be able to assert our position more. To say "No". To push for change. To be clear on what we feel is right.

Push yourself out of your comfort zone more, to have courageous conversations and build this as a habitual part of your behaviour and communication style. Sometimes the most difficult conversations are the ones most needed.

If you're in a leadership position, empower others and allow them to have a platform to express their views and opinions too.

k) Growth will be aided by a clear plan

Know what you're looking to achieve and develop a clear vision for this. Then build a more detailed plan of the tasks and steps needed to get there, including those of other people.

Understanding where you're trying to get to, how you will do this and by what date will build clarity for you and enable you to move from defensiveness to growth.

Willpower is all well and good, but a plan will support this in a practical way.

l) Take the next step

Once you have a plan, take the next step only. Don't get wrapped up in the myriad of things which need doing. But focus on the most important step you need to take today to move forwards on a project.

When I work with senior leaders and we develop a longer term strategy, I always bring it back to 90 day goals and then next steps for the following 2-4 weeks. Know the big picture, but keep focused on the most important steps to get there in the short term.

If you have hit challenges or blockers, focus on the next small step too. We often go defensive because the whole is too overwhelming. Take smaller steps to make progress.

m) Make public commitments

Making public commitments to others, especially if you're in a leadership role, will mean you're more likely to push through and make them happen. It can bring open accountability. When you hit roadblocks or mistakes, the urge to give up will be counter-balanced by your commitment.

I announced openly this book would be published April 11th 2024 over 6 months before, to ensure my defensive tendencies wouldn't allow me to miss the date. This public commitment helped move me out of defensive positions at many points on the journey.

You can also make stronger commitments with yourself and use the dopamine hits of rewards to push you through barriers on your journey to deliver against those commitments.

n) Analyse risk more objectively

It's good to be more rational and objective with all decisions which carry risk. For bigger projects, as I indicated earlier it's worth doing more elaborate risk analysis.

With risk analysis, you look at the likelihood of the risk occurring, the level of impact, how you can mitigate against this and how you would address the situation where the risk occurred. Analysis and a plan give a sense of control and calms our *survival psychology*.

o) Foster a growth culture

Build and nurture a culture within your organisation of having a collective growth mindset. Often blame cultures can develop and will quickly put people into a defensive and protective bubble. Shift the organisational mindset in the way mistakes and failure are dealt with well. Additionally develop healthy approaches to giving feedback which doesn't put people on the back foot and ensure everyone, from top down, is receptive to feedback.

For example, you can start with: "I want to give you some feedback on the recent project where there were some problems. The feedback is intended to help you learn and grow so you can handle future challenges more effectively".

Remember also the 3:1 ratio (from Marcial Losada) and ensure all the leaders in the organisation are giving much more positive feedback than they are probably doing currently. This is a key approach to moving people out of a *defensive mindset* when mistakes are made or challenges are faced.

Ask more questions as a way of releasing ideas and stimulating heathy debate. As touched on in relation to courageous conversations, people will often go quiet if they feel in any way threatened. Encourage those more withdrawn to share thoughts and ideas through the use of good questions.

Growth mindset organisations will have more trust, empowerment and ownership. Companies with a defensive culture will lose people. Know which side of the equation you want to be on and act accordingly.

p) Ensure there is a culture of psychological safety and inclusion

If people feel psychologically threatened by leaders or others within the organisation it can create a toxic and defensive culture.

Psychological safety (a term first used by Amy Edmondson and Harvard Business School) means people feel safe to speak up, to disagree openly, to air concerns without fear of negative repercussions or being put under pressure.

It's obvious any form of discrimination, labelling or stereotyping will counter both psychological safety and a growth culture. Inclusivity within your organisation will provide a framework of equality and fairness which will allow all to grow and realise their potential, regardless of their individual and group differences.

q) Promote and recruit people based on potential and mindset

Promote people based more on their potential and growth mindset, rather than them needing to be the finished article. Look at character and values, in terms of the people you promote or hire.

Invest in their growth but continually foster a mindset of growth in all as well. Leaders with a growth mindset will be committed to the development of their people through various routes – coaching, mentoring, training and self-study.

You could also follow the approach of some of my clients, where people are allocated a day or more a month to work on new skills or learning. They don't need to do this in their own time.

r) Understand and handle defence mechanisms

You may well observe any one of the defence mechanisms covered being demonstrated by others. Managing this needs you to develop and utilise coaching skills to shift the thinking and behaviour of others.

Whether it be projection, avoidance, lying, humour (which can very much be a destructive behaviour in teams through sarcasm and toxic banter) or any of the other defence mechanisms, become sharper at seeing them play out and deal with them. It may well mean individuals going through performance management if their behaviour does not change. Your values are highly unlikely to align with any of the defence mechanisms and so people demonstrating them will be going against your values.

s) Use the GROW coaching method

GROW was developed in the 1980s by Sir John Whitmore. When someone is stuck or has gone into their defensive bubble, it's important to take them through a set of questions to enable them to move to a place of growth

G - What is their GOAL or what are they trying to achieve?
R – What is the REALITY of where they are now?
O – What are their OPTIONS to move forwards?
W – What action WILL they take?

You can supplement these questions, but this is a great model to move people to a place of self-sufficiency and empowerment.

I have worked with many senior leaders who love this model, as it allows them to help their people become more self-sufficient, rather than fixing their problems for them.

t) Collective reflection

As well as doing individual reflection, carve out time in your diary every 3 months where your teams can reflect on where they are currently. What's been going well and what's not been going so well. Where are the blockers? You can apply this to projects to enable all to review progress. I'm also a great advocate of 'post implementation reviews' for larger projects. When I was a project manager, we would bring the people together who were involved in a project (sometimes including people who were external to our organisation), and we would discuss the things which went well and the things which didn't go so well in detail. We would take the lessons so we could build these into the future project work.

With all of your projects, particularly the ones which didn't go so well, don't let the culture of defensiveness take over.

u) 360-degree feedback

Even if your organisation does not do this formally, I strongly recommend you should do this if you're in a leadership role. Create a set of questions to gain feedback on how you're performing in your role and provide these to people in your team(s), the peer leaders at your level and the person you report into. Receiving feedback like this needs you to get yourself into a growth mindset more than ever, because the tendency to go defensive will be strong. It could make you feel threatened and even fear for your survival in your leadership position.

I remember doing this with one of my teams and one of the team members gave me his feedback document and said: "remember the most useful form of criticism is more critical in nature!". This put me on the backfoot for a moment, until I mindfully decided to take on board any comments which could help me grow as a leader and there were a number of those.

v) Don't lose sight of the positives

Among all the talk of challenges, failure, mistakes and critical feedback, let's not lose sight of the good which happens within and around us. We can learn from the more negative experiences, but we can also learn and embed the positive.

Often as leaders it's good to know our strengths and utilise these as best we can. As groups or organisations, paths using our collective strengths will often be the best to pursue.

Appreciative Inquiry is an approach from Positive Psychology. It's a way of looking at organisational change with a stronger focus on identifying and doing more of what is already working, rather than looking for problems and trying to fix them. It should be part of your culture and philosophy. Appreciating what you do well and utilising your strengths is a definite antidote to the *defensive mindset.*

Summary

- Our *survival psychology* will look to keep us safe and this can often lead to a need to protect ourselves from potential threats – physical, practical and psychological

- Mistakes, feedback, challenges and the need to make big decisions can lead to us going into defensive positions. Our self-esteem can feel vulnerable, and we look to defend it in any way we can

- Only by moving out of your protective bubble will we truly grow. Learning from mistakes, being open to critical feedback, remaining ready to learn new skills and making big decisions will all keep us moving forwards

- We can all consciously choose a path of growth, rather than going defensive

We've been examining how we can go into a protective bubble to defend ourselves. Let's move on now to look at the subject of *ego*, which is the way in which we can get pre-occupied with our own individual importance.

3. EGO

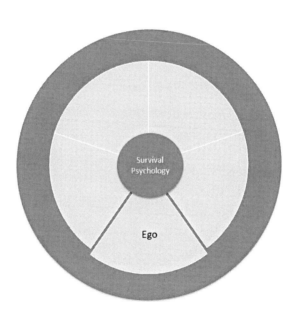

"Your ego will drive you to believe you are important and separate or it will continually strive to become important."

Views on ego

Ego is a manifestation of our *survival psychology*, as we seek to protect ourselves from threats and danger to keep us safe. Often in modern life, our survival thinking is less about our physical safety and more psychological in nature. It's focused on protecting our self-esteem and our *ego* is at the heart of this. *Ego* is predominantly driven by fear.

In a joint interview between Eckhart Tolle and Wayne Dyer (2 of the great writers on spirituality), Dyer joked about being ranked number 2 spiritual leader to Tolle at number 1. Being aware of the destructive power of *ego*, he joked that he still wanted to take the number 1 slot. Tolle said these kinds of accolades needed to be dropped like a hot stone!

This stayed with me.

In 2023 I interviewed Martin Ingham, CEO of Motorpoint, for my podcast series Leadership Mindset (episode 56). At the end of the interview I asked him what he would like his legacy to be. He said he would like to walk away and nobody notice any difference. Humility of this kind is not the language of *ego*!

This has stayed with me too.

Ego wants us to be important and often it will see threats to this aim from situations and other people. *Ego* impacts us in

2 distinct ways. It will either push us continually to achieve a higher level of importance or it will delude us we're more important than we truly are.

For many people *ego* will never be satisfied and will continually drive them to have more and be more. It will leave them with the lasting impact of never feeling good enough. It is a form of inferiority complex. This is the most common journey for the majority of us in relation to *ego*.

For others *ego*'s need for importance leads them to have over inflated views about themselves, which can lead to delusionary thoughts and behaviour. In this approach it is a form of superiority complex. It can also drive a level of complacency, where actions or work which needs doing to achieve challenging goals will not be done. *Ego* can also drive the pursuit of power and the abuse of power, due to the insatiable need for importance. At its extreme, *ego* can be significantly related to personality disorders. In fact, 1% of the population are psychopaths, with zero empathy and behaviour which is totally consumed with self-interest.

In either of these cases an egoist, or someone under the strong influence of their *ego*, will be focused on self, with little regard for others. In both cases *ego* wants more to satisfy the need for self-importance. It wants us to be better than we are. It wants us to be better than others. It wants us to have achieved more and own more. It wants us to feel we're 'not good enough', to drive us forwards or delude ourselves we're important.

Where are you in your relationship with your ego?

Are you continually in a place where you feel you haven't achieved enough? That you're not enough? Or that you don't have enough?

Feelings of this nature will lead you to the place where there is a lack of satisfaction with your present situation or you constantly feel the need to get somewhere else, instead of enjoying and embracing where you are.

Alternatively, do you feel *ego* has led you to have over inflated ideas about self? In this second scenario, your *ego* can become obsessed with your own level of importance and your status level. It will lead you to falsely convince yourself of your level of importance. A cognitive bias called the Dunning-Kruger effect captures this. This cognitive bias shows up where a person with limited competence in a particular area will overestimate their abilities. This can be technical or leadership. The Dunning-Kruger effect is very much linked with the superiority complex manifestation of *ego*.

As a leader, the need for importance will most likely leave you unhappy and unfulfilled in your role. It will leave you feeling inferior. The alternative scenario, where you convince yourself of your importance, will negatively impact on your relationships with your people. Due to your feelings of being superior, you will struggle to let others in and will fail to influence the direction of the team.

My relationship with my ego

Why am I writing this book?

I'd like to think it's not about seeking plaudits for writing my second book. It's not seeking to impress you with my knowledge. It certainly is not about fame and money! I have worked to consciously create something I feel will be both interesting and useful. Something which will help you change your life and the way you behave as a leader. I wanted to be of service to you and others.

I read many books leading up to writing this book and sometimes found myself doubting my ability or feeling I was inferior as a writer. But I knew it was my *ego*, driven by survival thinking, trying to protect me. It would have loved me not to have written this book, based on the *ego*'s fear of being exposed as 'not good enough', especially when compared with others.

As you will see my *ego* didn't win.

When I work as a leadership psychologist, I often share a link to my 60+ LinkedIn recommendations (here for you if you'd like to see them www.linkedin.com/in/tonybrooks63/details/recommendations) when someone is trying to decide whether to work with me. I focus on this being something useful to leaders to help them make the right decision for themselves. My *ego* could trip me up here and make it all about me and inflating my self-esteem, but I do my best to focus on purely being of service.

Definitions and Freud

There are a number of different definitions and interpretations of what *ego* actually means. As we go right back to the origins of the word with Freud, *ego* was seen to be the sense of self which balances between what Freud called the 'id' (and our emotional drives) and the 'super ego' (the moralistic views and rules which need to be followed). The *ego* was seen by Freud to serve the 3 masters - the 'super ego', the 'id' and additionally having to deal with the external real world. In this view, *ego* needs to find a balance between those primitive drives, the limitations imposed by reality and the constraints of the 'super ego'.

In Freud's model, the *ego* employs a whole raft of defence mechanisms to keep the person safe, including denial, projection and repression. These are often counterproductive and although designed to keep the person safe from anxiety, deny growth (we looked at these in more detail in the *defensive mindset* chapter).

Perceptions of *ego* have evolved over time. For me, *ego* is the voice in my head which continually seeks to increase my importance and challenges me when I'm perceived to be less important than I should be or in comparison with other people.

I very much relate to Eckhart Tolle's view of *ego* (in the book 'New Earth'*)*. Tolle sees it being a fixation on self through the egoic mind, based on the false self and the person we truly are not. The person we're continually striving to be rather than who we truly are.

Self-esteem and self-worth

I have used the term self-esteem in relation to *ego* and it's worth distinguishing this and self-worth. Self-esteem refers to your assessment of your abilities, accomplishments and validation by the external world. Self-worth is a deeper view on your worth and value as a human being. Self-esteem can vary based on external validation and circumstances and I see this as being more in line with ego. Self-worth is a more stable belief and less conditional. It links to the important point I have made about seeing yourself as intrinsically 'good enough' as a person.

The things we seek in order to bolster ego

Materialism can be a key factor in bolstering *ego* and self-esteem. We buy more and more 'identity enhancers' including jewellery, top brands, expensive cars and bigger and better homes. We often look to make ourselves more important through our achievements too, such as qualifications or accolades. We may also seek to bolster our self-esteem through association with other people we perceive to be important. It can even mean looking for the love of another or a relationship to inflate our own *ego*.

It's an endless path of greed to seek more and more validation… and it has no end!

A lesson from Frasier

One of the best observations on *ego* was an episode of Frasier (which in my humble opinion is the greatest comedy of all time).

Frasier (who is the lead character if you've not watched the program) and his brother Niles heard about a new health club and they managed to pull some strings to get into the club. They then found out there was an elevated level of membership, the gold membership, which they became obsessed with aspiring to. They used a friend with contacts to enable them to get to the gold level. It clearly wasn't just about the experience; it was validation for who they were as people.

Once they were in a very luxurious environment in the gold membership level, they spotted …a platinum door! Niles quickly became obsessed with going through the platinum door to the perceived higher level of membership he now felt was more befitting their status.

Frasier asked Niles "Why is it we can't be happy with where we are Niles. Why must we let something which can only be incrementally better ruin the here and now? I'm through chasing the eternal carrot!" (good thought!)

But once told they could not go through the door, they were both gripped by the need to aspire to a higher level. When they finally managed to find a way through the platinum door, they discovered it was actually just a door out into the refuse area and they got locked out of the health club!

What a fantastic observation on how the *ego* can hijack us all. *Ego* will encourage you to aspire higher and look down on others. It's also an underlying influence on class-based systems and snobbery.

A focus on 'I' or 'We'

We have an important fork in the road to reflect on as we continue our journey. Should our path be about 'I' or 'We'?

The *ego* will seek to separate us from other people. It'll want to be self-sufficient and elevate us above other people. It will continually strive to prove our individual importance. It will ultimately isolate us and keep us fixated on the 'I'. There is an element of this needed to start businesses or drive new strategies, but the journey from there will be much more productive by collaborating with others.

We achieve our best work collectively, as I will discuss further in this chapter and the group behaviour chapter. When we move from the 'I' to the 'We' it loosens *ego*'s grip. It takes our focus from being inwards to being outwards. It makes us more human and connected. It will create more purpose and meaning and will achieve so much more!

The '3 Toxic Cs'

As we continue to gain a clearer understanding of how *ego* can undermine us, let me introduce you to the '3 Toxic Cs'.

Ego impacts us via '3 Toxic Cs'.

Criticising	We seek to elevate ourselves by criticising other people. At its worst we continually criticise ourselves due to *ego*'s vision of us. Or we feel that where we are currently doesn't match up to where the *ego* believes we should be (and the word 'should' is very much the language of the *ego*!).
Complaining	Here we complain all the time because we want to look for factors which justify why we aren't living up to the level created for us by our *ego*. We complain about our situation, we complain about other people, we blame other people, we insult other people, we resent other people's progress. All of this forms a way of thinking where we don't feel we are in the place we should be. We complain to strengthen our own *ego* and playing the victim justifies our position and our potential lack of action.
Competing	We can end up endlessly competing or comparing ourselves to others. To elevate our sense of self and raise our level of importance means we will be looking for others we need to take on and beat. We

need to win and only by doing this will our *ego* be fulfilled. An element of competition in life can be healthy, but it can also take us on a path which is fruitless and a never-ending journey. We don't compete with people beneath us and the many people in less fortunate positions. We don't compete with people at the same level. We continually compete with the people who we perceive to be in a better place than us. The word perceive is critical here, because often our perception of somebody else's position is very different from their reality or their perception of where they are. *Ego* leads to envy and it doesn't matter how well you're doing, your *ego* and the accomplishments of others will make you feel small and inferior. Your *ego* will want you to either make moves to improve and get beyond these people or it will want you to take them down. At its worst this can result in backstabbing, corrupt behaviour or the will to do harm to others.

Criticising, complaining and competing can be used often with the aim of raising one's own importance. Either to drive you on a journey to reach a level of importance your *ego* feels is justifiably yours or to delude you with an overinflated idea about your own capability in order to convince you of your importance.

Ego and relationships

Ego can also impact our relationships with other people. *Ego* will always want something from other people to reach a higher level and it nearly always has a hidden agenda. *Ego* will associate with others, seek the love of others, take people down. Its focus is selfish. The '3 Toxic Cs' will greatly influence our relationships with other people.

Ego seeks to be important and will see the opportunity to do this via relationships with others. Ultimately, *ego* needs us to be important as it believes this will keep us safe and it can drive us to use people and situations to get what it feels is needed. The trouble is, even when we succeed, the *ego* is never satisfied and not happy for very long.

Your *ego* will typically mistrust other people. It will see them as a potential threat on your path to an increased level of importance. It will look to use them or take them down. Awareness of this is a key antidote, along with a focus on strong core values. We need to understand the fears and drives of *ego* to manage it more effectively.

Note also that the *ego* of others may well have a hidden agenda. Building bridges with people, by shifting out of your *ego* and allowing them to do same will help with this. We also need to remain aware and vigilant of how their *ego* may be playing out and could impact you.

The language of ego

Look out for the words of *ego,* both in your communication with others and especially with self. *Ego* will continually hit you with the word 'should', leading to you feeling you are inadequate when related things are not done. Other words which will seep into your inner dialogue are 'win', 'failure', 'compete', 'judge', 'hate'. If *ego* takes over your inner dialogue it will either make you feel 'not good enough' or it will try to convince you you're way more important than you truly are. It needs you to be important and either strategy can be employed.

Bridging the gap

Ego looks at the gap between where we are and where it believes we should be (the word 'should' again) and this kind of thinking will drive us to a place where we don't feel good enough.

We have an underlying fear of being nobody and not being important. *Ego* will drive us to a place of insecurity, if it feels we don't have the status needed. Alternatively, it can put us in a place of complacency, if it feels we have achieved the status.

Most of what we do through *ego* is only actually a cover up or temporary. It will never be truly satisfied or secure. Only by accepting ourselves for who we really are will we be able to start on a healthier path. Acknowledging we are good at our core and that we're aspiring to grow will begin to liberate us from *ego*'s grip.

One of the biggest 'elephants in the room' is most people are undermined by their *ego* continuously. They don't feel good enough in areas of their life, both personal and professional. It can be difficult to open up about this to others, so they aren't as truthful with themselves or others as they could be.

Delusion and personality disorders

As touched on earlier, *ego* can take people to a place of delusion, which can often be accompanied by personality disorders, such as narcissism. Antisocial personality disorders include being a sociopath or even a psychopath. As before, it's said there are circa 1 in 100 people who have psychopathic tendencies, it's also been found in research by the American Psychological Association that close to 30% of us have some level of psychopathic traits!

The research also found 1.2% of US adult men, and up to 0.7% of US adult women were considered to have clinically significant levels of psychopathic traits. It's highly likely you're dealing with people in your organisations who may have psychopathic traits. The *ego* of these people can be very destructive.

This extreme end of the *ego* spectrum is where there is no consideration for others or their feelings. It is completely about the person who is engulfed in self and achieving what they want, whatever the cost. In fact, many of the disorders we're talking about consist of the same egoic traits which operate in a normal person, except they become so pronounced they're pathological.

Many of us tell lies from time to time to appear more important or special. Some people, driven by *ego*, will lapse into this more habitually and compulsively and it's where we start to move into the area of personality disorders.

Healthy ego

The extremes of *ego* are linked to personality disorders, but can *ego* ever be healthy? Many of you will believe an element of *ego* is healthy and it will drive you forwards to achieve more. There is no big issue with this, if it's the way you choose to lead your life and career. It will continually leave you in a place of lack and a feeling you haven't fulfilled your potential, but I understand why this course is often chosen.

It also links to the Idea of 'healthy narcissism' (yes, narcissism is not universally seen as something bad!). Dr Elinor Greenberg, in her book 'Borderline, Narcissistic and Schizoid Adaptions', described this as "a sense of positive self-regard based on a realistic understanding and self-acceptance of one's own strengths and weaknesses".

If you wish to pursue a path of healthy *ego* and narcissism, it's worth keeping those thoughts as a guide.

Let's take a deeper look at some factors relating to *ego* and its influence on the behaviour and thinking of leaders.

Introversion and extraversion

There's been a continual debate over time about the difference between introverts and extroverts. The discourse about personality differentiators originates from the work of Carl Jung, but it's been made more famous via psychometric tools like Myers Briggs.

In recent years I've worked with a range of leaders who exist at various points on the spectrum of introversion to extraversion and all have the ability to be great leaders regardless. It's interesting to relate to Jim Collins' book *Good to Great*. One of the key findings in his research, looking at 28 highly successful companies over 30 years, was they were predominantly led by introverts. In the book, Collins looked at various levels of leadership right up to what he termed level 5 - 'Executive'. The 'Executive' level is where leaders build enduring greatness by humility. It's humility which can be a strong counter to the drive of *ego*. Acceptance of the fact that we are not any more important than another person and able to achieve things working with others. Level 5 leaders will first and foremost think about the success of their organisation and their people over their own personal ambition.

Typically, these are leaders who are more reserved in nature, but show fierceness and determination in getting the job done. They think about the future of their companies without them, and plan about their succession. Humility like this directly relates to the example I was talking about with Martin Ingham as CEO for the Motorpoint Arena in Nottingham. Level 5 leaders are generally more modest, and they don't like to talk about themselves or their achievements. They prefer to share the credit with others rather than being more self-obsessed, egalitarian and focused on fulfilling the needs of their *ego*.

In times of failure, level 5 leaders usually take responsibility. The opposite is the case for leaders driven by their *ego*. They will look to point the finger at others.

The impact of ego on communication

We looked at *ego* and relationships earlier, but I want to explore another concept which is insightful for leaders when communicating with their people. Let's examine the ideas of transactional analysis, first formulated by American psychiatrist Eric Bern in 1958. People take different positions (influenced by *ego)* when communicating with others and these can help or hinder the relationship. His view was that there were 3 'ego states' which we can move into in our relationships with others:

'Parent ego state'	Taken from the attitudes and behaviours of parents and other significant figures in the environment, which could include teachers and figures of authority (there's a link to the 'super ego' in Freud's model here).
'Child ego state'	Based on the feelings, attitudes and behaviours which have come about from the person's past.
'Adult ego state'	Where feelings, attitudes and behaviors are more of a direct response to the here and now reality. The adult state is when we're more attentive to the present, we're able to evaluate pros and

	cons and be more rational. We gather data and information and ask questions reasonably logically. It is said the state develops very early in children from the age of 10 months.

It's interesting to look at the way people interrelate when they get into the different ego states and positions. The most constructive way we can communicate is when both people are in the 'adult ego state'. However, when somebody is angry with you, if you go to a 'parent ego state', this can lead to confrontational communication or we can go to the 'child ego state', where we go more passive or play the role of a victim. What is really needed is to go to the adult state, to be present in the here and now and to understand what has made the person angry so we can look to resolve this.

In a broader sense, communication will be significantly impacted by the *ego*s of individuals. If the *ego* is strong in somebody and feels unfulfilled, it's highly likely any communication will be more destructive rather than constructive in nature.

The mind-traps leaders face with ego

I've observed and heard about many examples of *ego* playing out for leaders through time:

- A single person's *ego* detrimentally impacting the culture of the team or whole organisation
- Senior people feeling threatened by the ideas of other senior leaders or other people within the organisation.
- A fear of letting ourselves down
- There being many people in the same industry leading to feelings of being inferior
- Feeling threatened when someone of high caliber joins the team
- Losing motivation when things don't go as expected or desired
- Someone taking over a role during maternity leave leading to insecurity

This is just the tip of the iceberg of the ways in which *ego* can damage leaders and their people. I'm sure you'll relate to one or more of the real-life examples above or have examples of your own if you are open and honest.

We all must arrive at our own view of what *ego* means to us individually and whether we see this as problematic, empowering, healthy or destructive to ourselves and to others.

Ego causes problems throughout society. Starting wars at its worst. We also see examples of corruption, abuse of power, road rage and often *ego* is the trigger for infidelity in our personal lives. The impact of *ego* in personal, professional and global relationships is apparent for all to see.

Let's explore further challenges for leaders gripped by *ego*.

Ego in leadership

Let's talk about how *ego* can play out more specifically in leadership roles, both hindering a leader and impacting the people within the organisation.

The problem with an unfulfilled *ego* is that achievements and progress made are not appreciated or recognised. It wants more. It could be a promotion, a new position in a different company, more qualifications. I see this play out in the endless need to fulfil *ego* in my experiences both working with leaders and within organisations.

Leaders and others look to fulfil their *ego*, continually looking for the next step up. They become preoccupied with job titles, or qualifications and they never have enough and strive for more. They may become preoccupied with the number of people they manage or fixated on other matters. In the craziest example I've seen in a company I worked for, there was a fixation and obsession with whether an individual had a parking space and what kind of parking space it was!

Ego will lead us on a path to never feeling like we have enough money, enough material possessions or a high enough position. Winning becomes everything and coming second a failure. I interviewed Andrea Pinchen (episode 50), the CEO of Leicester Tigers, for my podcast series Leadership Mindset, not long after they'd won the Rugby Premiership in 2022. It was interesting for me to hear her response when I asked her how she would feel if they didn't win the Premiership the following season.

I asked: "How would it feel if you came second next time?" She said this would be okay, although she would like to see progress in other aspects of the club, which could have been off the field and things they were doing around conferencing. In the end, they came third and I'm still not sure what Andrea made of this! But what a great example of where somebody can keep their *ego* and need to come first in check.

The trappings of ego

Ego can lead us on an endless pursuit for more likes on social media and interaction with our posts. How many of us put posts out on the various platforms whether it be TikTok, Threads, X, Instagram, LinkedIn or Facebook, only to continually monitor whether people are interested in what we have said in an attempt to fluff our own sense of self-importance.

The path of fame can create enormous problems with *ego*. If left unchecked, it can drive people to behaviour which is extremely inappropriate. We can only imagine what it might be like for somebody with a significant level of fame. The inner battle they must have with their own *ego* as to whether they have made the level which is acceptable, or they feel the need to go higher (clue here – it's probably the latter).

For leaders in organisations, the inner battle with *ego* can play out too, even if on a smaller scale. The continual path of needing more and more power, higher status, more rewards. Know again it's highly likely your *ego* will never be satisfied.

It's better for ourselves and others to focus on humility, being humble, working with other people to achieve things. Then work on yourself to have the courage to defer to others when things are achieved. Finding this is a healthier path for you and for others.

The '3 Toxic Cs' in leadership

Leaders can be undermined by the '3 Toxic Cs' of *ego* I described earlier. Criticising, Complaining and Competing.

- A leader will continually criticise their people and this can lead to a blame culture where people are fearful of making mistakes or being open about them
- A leader will complain, leading to a lack of responsibility being taken or ownership of the work which needs doing to grow
- A leader will compete with others at the same level or higher in an attempt to raise their own status. They will become pre-occupied with status symbols too

I found it amusing when I was at a networking event several years back, where a coach was having a conversation with a woman who had moved into a senior management position. He said it was about time she had a BMW. In his eyes the ultimate status symbol and a validation for her position.

On the competition front you may find you continually compare and vie with others in your industry. We need healthy competition and we need to be aware of the competition, but this can become destructive or all encompassing. I've spoken with several business owners who shared their continual need to focus on the competition. For example, I spoke with someone running an HR business where they admitted they gave too much attention to how their business compares with other HR businesses. But often a focus on what you're doing and your growth is more fruitful, including work to differentiate yourself for sure. You may also be missing a trick to collaborate with other people in your area of work, which I'm pleased to say I've done on a number of occasions (including many guests on my podcast show).

Being right

The problem in organisations when *ego* takes hold, is that being right becomes especially important. It means either somebody else needs to be wrong or the situation needs to be wrong. When one *ego* goes into battle with another the results are nearly always destructive.

Being right can be a collective problem too, where you get a group of people or a team forming an 'egoic entity'. They will unify in not admitting their failings and point their collective finger at other parts of the organisation if put on the back foot. The need to be right for the group directly relates to the form of silo behaviour which will be covered in the *group behaviour* chapter.

The need to be right can destroy relationships between individuals and teams. It often ultimately means both sides lose.

Control

Ego will need to have control over the threats which are coming or potential threats. At its centre it is still fear based, which leaves it on an impossible quest and a preoccupation with control. The need for control will mean leaders don't relate well to other people in the organisation, there is little trust and there's a reluctance to delegate and release control of anything! The best leaders I have found, through my experience, are more able to release control. They don't see the need for power through control or status.

The need for control or not being seen to have been wrong can also lead to a fruitless path of 'not letting go' of something which isn't working anymore. A system the leader decided on, a person recruited, a product idea. I have also witnessed leaders staying in roles for too long, feeling obligated to make it work when it's evident, for various reasons, that they have reached the end of the line.

The abuse of power

The path to wanting more control is also linked to the desire for power. A greater position of power will give a leader more control. There are many examples of where power has been abused, from the sexual abuse claims made against Jimmy Saville right the way through to Commodus the Roman Emperor (from 177 to 192).

The Roman Senate tried to write Commodus out of history once he died, such was the level of his impact. He was described by ancient historian Cassius Dio as being "a greater curse to Romans than any pestilence or crime". Destructive dictatorships have had horrific consequences for people within and outside countries throughout time.

Destructive leaders have abused their power in businesses too, including the failure of HP CEO Carly Fiorina (after trying to buy Price Waterhouse at a significantly inflated price) and Ken Lay (at Enron).

Vulnerability

All forms of *ego* can make it incredibly difficult to share our vulnerability and fears. Your *ego* won't want you to admit you're fallible or vulnerable. It will prefer the paths of control and power just highlighted. But vulnerability is just an awareness of being human and fallible and being more open about what is going on within self. Your *ego* will not want you to share your psychological battles and can lead many people to secretly try and handle mental health conditions alone.

Mental health conditions resulting from this are especially problematic for men (around 75% of suicides are carried out by men according to ONS UK). In the classic, stereotypical view, men are seen to need to be strong in times of difficulty. Sharing vulnerability can be especially hard for men, but this is so important across the spectrum of humankind. It's heart breaking that the needs of the *ego* can lead many people to commit suicide and take their own lives (5,275 in the UK in 2022 – ONS UK).

As a leader, if you show vulnerability, it can help others to do the same. It's part of being an authentic human leader. There are many times when people need you to be strong, even if you feel insecure, but they also need to be able to show their vulnerability and you being prepared to do this at the right time will help them do the same.

Going it alone

You may realise deep down you need help, rather than continuing to plough your path alone. *Ego* won't support you doing this as it doesn't want you to appear vulnerable. Due to issues around control, self-esteem, and the need to be number one, your *ego* will want you to achieve and take credit for things independently. The notion of doing things with the assistance, support and collaboration of other people, becomes unacceptable to *ego*. Other people are seen as untrustworthy, competition or a threat.

However, we know many hands can make for more effective work (as I will cover more in the *group behaviour* chapter). Reach out and ask for help, even if you're the head of a company. If other people have the skills in your team you don't have, don't feel threatened as you don't need to know it all. There are people within and outside your company who can often help you solve your problems. *Ego* wants you to go it alone and can isolate you, but you can achieve much more working collectively.

Being deluded rather than doing the work

For some leaders, *ego* can bring an overinflated view of self, which directly relates to a cognitive bias known as 'overconfidence bias'. These individuals slide into an *ego* state where they believe they are better than others and don't need others. They aren't realistic in their assessment of their abilities and current skill levels. They become totally self-absorbed with their own needs and wants.

Ego needs to be important. We will either continually strive (and fail) to achieve this or delude ourselves we are important. It can be especially dangerous after we have achieved something of note. There are many leaders in organisations who are delusional about their own ability levels (and fall foul of the 'Dunning Kruger' bias). There are those too who have ended up in leadership positions and don't necessarily have the right skills, but find it difficult to admit their own fallibility and their need for help. At the extreme, the delusional *ego* can destroy organisations and it can destroy the growth of organisations. Confidence is important to build. Delusional *ego* is to be avoided at all costs.

I remember having a call with the HR manager in 2020, where she spoke of the head of the company so consumed with his *ego,* constrained the ability of the company to grow, as he made isolated decisions and lacked trust in anyone to take responsibility. This meant their revenue potential was held back and new developments were thwarted.

Damaged ego

Nothing can separate us or be as toxic as a damaged *ego*. Resentment, anger, hate can grip someone who feels wronged and they will not let go of this. Feeling wronged can lead to an all-consuming preoccupation with the past and the wrong done. It can mean the person seeks vengeance, which can be harmful for both parties or it can just sap the time and energy of the person whose *ego* has been damaged.

Avoidance

Ego wants to keep us safe and protect our status. The result is that any tasks or actions which could lead to us making mistakes, failing or show us up as being foolish, will be avoided if *ego* has its say. It can sap the fun out of life and deny you growth.

I have worked with leaders who hold back on new ideas or making suggestions for changes, simply because they are concerned of the reaction. If the culture doesn't accept this, you need to influence the culture or part ways.

How to escape the mind-traps of ego

* Mindset

As with all the mind-traps of *survival psychology* in this book, conscious awareness is even more critically important in relation to *ego*. Eckhart Tolle, in his book 'New Earth', spoke about the notion *ego* cannot exist when we are fully aware. Conscious awareness of what is going on will allow you to shine a light on your *ego* and diminish its power.

Only from this place of conscious awareness can we start to expose the destructive nature of *ego*, on its continual path to seek greater importance. It is a manifestation of the 'destructive self' I described in the introduction and its destruction can be to self, others and organisations.

Know also your *ego* will never be satisfied. It will want to have and be more. Only the 'true you' can challenge this. Be present, be realistic, be rational and focus on your journey of growth. Some training or education in mindfulness may support you with this.

Also be mindful of reacting to the *ego* in others. We saw this in relation to the 3 'ego states' in the transactional analysis model. However, in a general sense when you see *ego* occurring in others, whether this be from a place of their continual need to be right or to be important, don't react and fuel it.

* Practical tools and actions for you

Here are a number of practical tools and actions which will support you in relation to *ego*. Select the 1 or 2 you feel addresses your biggest challenges and focus on these first.

a) Ask yourself why?

Firstly, when you are seeking to do something or achieve something new ask yourself why? Why do you need to achieve more? Why do you need more? Why are you in competition? If you don't ask yourself these questions your *ego* will default to needing more. There may be good answers which justify what you're looking to do, but ensure they are the right reasons.

When I'm in coaching situations and somebody talks to me about aspiring to another level, taking on a new or additional role or seeking to achieve more qualifications such as an MBA, I ask them: why? Why is it important? What will it deliver? Ask yourself those questions, as you may just be on a path to attempt to fulfil your *ego* (which is a path you won't win!). Make sure your aspirations are truly the right ones for you.

b) Use the '3 Empowering As'

When you find you're being tripped up by the '3 Toxic Cs' of *ego*, look at the '3 Empowering As' to mitigate this:

'Acknowledge'	Rather than criticise others and self, acknowledge the path of growth will always be paved with mistakes along the way for everyone.
'Accept'	Diminish the need to complain and accept the situation you find yourself and your responsibility for this. Push yourself to act to do something about it.
'Appreciate'	Rather than compete (and compare) with other people, appreciate what you've done on your journey so far. None of us take stock of what we've achieved enough, as I mentioned in the chapter on *impostor syndrome* (see your Success, Skills & Strengths Script).

c) Make realistic self-assessments

To develop the last point above, periodically make a realistic assessment of your skills, strengths and areas which need work. Know you're on a path of growth, but avoid becoming delusional with the trappings of the 'overconfidence bias'. You're going to need to work hard to achieve the things you want to achieve and *ego* won't buy into this! Also be comfortable shining a light on failures and mistakes, especially if you are responsible. Take the learnings, grow and do things differently. Continually help others to do the same too.

I appreciate this is tough to do but know when it's right for you to take a step down. I've seen many people continue on a path of stress and turmoil, when they have reached a level beyond their capabilities and strengths or they just plain don't enjoy it!

If you can't get the development needed to improve or you don't really want the role you're doing, put your *ego* to one side and do the right thing for you. Ambition is all well and good, but not if it makes you unhappy and damages your health.

d) Focus on values

Become much more focused on your own values rather than the need to achieve and win all the time.

Don't be sucked in by *ego* and the '3 Toxic Cs' but do the right thing in line with your values. Being guided by your values includes the way you relate to other people. Recognise when you're in conflict with your values or acting in a way which is not in accordance with those values. *Ego* will not respect values; it will just see you need to move to a higher level.

e) Focus on internal validation

Focus more on internal versus external validation. *Ego* will be driven by the need for external validation in all its forms, including accolades and praise. Your values are a key part of the internal validation which will keep you more grounded. Detaching from external validation will do the same for you.

Be more like Eckhart Tolle and drop accolades like a hot stone (although you may want to use them in your marketing). Be more like the long list of people who have declined OBEs (Dawn French, Nigella Lawson, Bill Nighy, Benjamin Zephaniah) or Grammys (Marlon Brando, Sinead O'Connor) and don't let your *ego* get unnecessarily sucked in with unimportant awards.

Focus on the internal feelings (and behaviour in line with your values) rather than the external material rewards and accolades. Sometimes it's just about taking stock that you're doing good work and you're making progress without any real need for external manifestation. *Ego* wants results speedily and will be fed by winning and achievements, but often it doesn't have to work like this.

f) Stay humble

We've seen this in the examples from Jim Collins and his book Good to Great. With the people declining OBEs and Grammys in part e) above. With Martin Ingham. Even Einstein, one of the greatest Physicists in the world, was known to be very humble.

I'm not the greatest leadership psychologist in the world. I'm not the greatest author, speaker or trainer in the world, but I feel I'm good at what I do and I'm always looking to learn from others, from experiences and to grow further.

Whether you're a senior leader, an MD or a CEO, wherever you are on your leadership journey, progress from a place of humility. Recognise how well you've done to get to this place and then know there are many options and ways in which you can continue to grow. Ironically, letting your *ego* get in the way of this will stop you from taking some of those paths which can help you grow and improve more anyway! Make the right choices on your path of growth.

Be confident in the skills, knowledge and experience you have, but remain humble. Humility also needs you to admit you are wrong, to compromise and to apologise. This will strengthen the relationships you have, both personal and professional. Humility also needs us to show more gratitude and appreciation for others. The more you recognise people's progress, hard work and achievements, the higher their performance will be (but be mindful of not feeding their individual *egos*).

g) Admit your mistakes and failures

Ego will be especially harsh on you when you make mistakes or fail. Here's the thing though - we all make them! The most successful people on the planet have all made mistakes, big ones. They are part of the journey of growth (and we explored this a lot more in the chapter on *defensive mindset*). *Ego* will either want you to get wrapped up in the feeling life has been unfair or blame others for a perceived slight (known as a narcissistic injury). Alternatively, it will be harsh on you and want you to withdraw from the threat of this happening again. It takes you back to your comfort zone, where your status can't be challenged.

Ego can also keep you on the wrong path, for fear of admitting you made a wrong choice. It wants you to be right at all costs. Don't listen to it. Learn from mistakes, change direction, seek feedback, draw a line and go forwards.

h) Be an eternal student

For different aspects of your role seek the wisdom of others to improve yourself. Read, attend webinars, work with mentors, study topics, attend training and have a persistent thirst to learn. You will never be the finished article (your *ego* will be very unsettled by this statement), but you can continually grow and improve. Others know more and this is nothing to be fearful of. Work with others to improve and achieve your goals more successfully.

The first thing Kirk Hammett did when he landed the role of lead guitarist with Metallica was to seek out a tutor – Joe Satriani. The first thing I did when I wanted to become a TEDx speaker was to be coached by someone who had been a TEDx speaker and curator (thank you Helen Packham!).

i) Abundance versus scarcity mentality

I started my business in 2007 and I have met a number of leadership psychologists and others doing similar work to me over the years. Rather than be triggered by the need to compare and compete, what I've attempted to do when I meet other people in similar professions is to engage with them and continually see what we can learn from each other or how we can support each other. I have ended up going into partnership with others, working on joint projects, interviewed 'competitors' for my podcast show and I have gained many friendships with people doing similar things to myself. From the start my *ego* was very unsettled by this and wanted to compete, but there are many people out there who need help and so I prefer to keep focused on the abundance of opportunity rather than let my *ego* convince me the opportunities are scarce and I need to be in a place of fear and competition.

j) Know what to say NO to

FOMO (Fear Of Missing Out) will lead you to say yes too often and lead you to do things which aren't important, compromising your ability to do other more valuable things. If your *ego* thinks this is an opportunity others (especially if it's the 'competition') are taking and will put you at a perceived disadvantage, it will not allow you to say NO.

Saying NO can also be compromised by the need to please or be validated by others. All of us waste precious time doing things we don't really need to out of fear or the need for endorsement of others.

Everyone can buy into the myth "if only I had that or was there then I'd be happy". But *ego* will then move the goal post. Say NO more often and keep focused on what you are doing now.

k) Distributed leadership

As I noted in relation to vulnerability, there is great wisdom, knowledge and experience throughout your teams and organisations which you can use more if you allow yourself to do this. It's also important you push back against your *ego* and relinquish control more. Delegate and share responsibility for tasks, projects and getting things done. It will be good for you and good for the people given more responsibility.

In some businesses a traditional hierarchy may suit it, but often the power can be devolved and your people can be involved through greater ownership. Your *ego* wants you to be a 'top dog', but this is almost always constraining and limits the ability to grow for your organisation, your people and ultimately yourself. You will achieve more moving from the 'I' to the 'We'.

l) Go to the 'OK Corral'

As touched on earlier, transactional analysis defines 3 'ego states'. A healthy and happy form of communication is when both participants come from a place of feeling they are ok and this is typified by both people being in the 'adult ego state'. Transaction Analysis rests on the belief that people are fundamentally okay, as Eric Berne established. To have more productive discussions as a leader, it is important to view yourself and others as okay.

m) Make people aware of their ego

Finally, notice when *ego* is playing out in others and know this will be mostly driven from a place of fear. Stroke another person's *ego* carefully and tactfully and make them aware when their *ego* is holding them or others back. It's going to take some skills and sensitivity to do this but allow people the space to become more aware of their own *ego* and see its destructive capability.

Summary

- *Ego* is ultimately fear based. It wants to protect your self-esteem and it will be continually monitoring for threats to this

- *Ego* wants you to be important and that is invariably important in relation to other people. It will either keep pushing you to become more important or delude you that you are more important than you truly are

- Being influenced too strongly by your *ego* will lead you to become more separate and isolated from others, but you will be much happier and successful working collectively

- Avoid the trappings of *ego* in all their forms (material, accolades, financial) and keep asking yourself why you need more

- Be mindful of the '3 Toxic Cs' and how they can trip you up and look to move to the '3 Empowering As'.

It's time to move from the challenges for the individual with *ego*, to the actions which can stem from *group behaviour*, both good and bad.

4. GROUP BEHAVIOUR

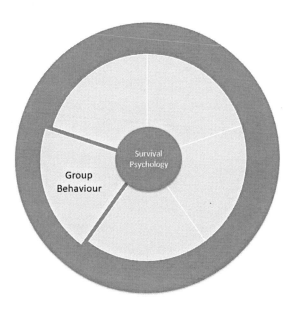

"We have a survival-based instinct to belong to groups. In modern life this can play out in positive ways, but it can also be very detrimental."

We have always needed to be part of a group

If we go back to the origins of the Homo species 2 million years ago, roaming the African savanna, their need for survival drove them to be part of close-knit tribes or groups. Having a leader who could lead them to safety and keep them safe was also paramount. All of this kept them alive.

Fast forward to modern life and we're still very much group orientated. Leadership, followership and team-ship have always been fundamental to our survival. As Seth Godin said in his book 'Tribes', "Human Beings can't help it, we need to belong and one of the most powerful or our survival mechanisms is to be part of a tribe".

What groups are you part of? It could be your family, groups of friends, a sporting team you follow, your ethnic group, your gender, your sexual identity, your work team, a number of social media groups you're part of. When you stand back it's incredible how many groups you are part of.

We gravitate towards groups in a multitude of different ways and although we may not be fully aware of it in modern life, there is still a deep-rooted part of our primitive psychology which looks for safety through being part of a group.

This is supported by several theories in psychology such as social learning theory, social constructionist theory and social identity theory. We are social and wired to connect.

Leadership (and followership) kept tribes alive for the origins of our species, and leadership is still seen as important today, to keep us safe both physically and psychologically. As a leader it's vital for you to be aware of how group behaviour can play out in your teams and organisations.

The evolution of the brain and how it relates to modern life

Within evolutionary theories and the work of Darwin, human behaviour is seen to be a product of the interaction between genes and environment. Our instincts can be modified by experience. We're in a continual to-ing and fro-ing of gene and environment interactions. Although we're partially determined by our genes, it's also about the context in which we find ourselves. Our interactions with our environment and our interactions with other people influence our behaviour. There have been some dramatic changes to the environments we have inhabited over time, which have had a significant impact.

The Homo brain volume has increased from about 400 cm^3 over 2 million years ago to 1350 cm^3 in modern times, but there is still a mismatch between the complexity of the modern world and some of the primitive functioning of our brain, which is still wired to handle the challenges faced by our ancestors. This mismatch has continued to develop over the years for our species.

We have been through some key shifts over time, the first being the agricultural revolution around 13,000 years ago. This resulted in larger settlements, greater hierarchies, less food scarcity and freed people to develop skills such as tool making.

A further big shift was the sequence of industrial revolutions, starting 250 years ago with the first Industrial Revolution (a transition to more efficient manufacturing processes). The second (technological), third (digital) and fourth (AI) industrial revolutions have increased the pace of change. This has all liberated people to be more mobile, with no need to stay within their geographical groups.

These shifts have caused a mismatch between modern organisations and leadership, when we compare it with the kind of leadership that the more primitive parts of our brains are still wired for. Our brain is still playing catch up!

The theory of anthropologist Dunbar, holds we can only really maintain about 150 connections at once. We are wired to be part of small groups and historically, groups of people used to be local. Fast forward and the internet has changed all this massively. There are however limitations on the group size we can function with effectively and modern complex organisations and technology can provide challenges for our more primitive thinking and survival tendencies.

We have evolved and the environments we live in have changed dramatically. Still our need to be part of a group is strong and it can be a force for good, but it can be destructive in nature too.

Group behaviour as a force for good and bad

A recent 2023 UK survey by the Chartered Management Institute found almost one-third of UK workers have quit their job because of a negative workplace culture.

Within organisations, your teams will be as strong as the culture of its people. Your *group behavio*ur will be the foundation for how successful your organisation or teams will be. We are truly better together and aligned, but we also need to take account of all the ways *group behaviour* can divide us.

We see this in wider society, with the various forms of discrimination including racism, misogyny, ableism, homophobia and transphobia. It can also include a sense of belonging through cults and conspiracy theories. There are many ways we can create conflict between groups.

In organisations, this will include the feelings of 'us and them' divides between management and employees, discrimination, silo behaviour between teams and it can also include breakaway toxic groups, led by individuals with underhand and destructive goals.

We will be coming to all these areas in more detail, but have faith when we're connected, aligned and we work as a powerful collective, we can achieve so much more than when we function as unhealthy groups of individuals impacted by the downsides of *group behaviour* I've been describing.

How people function within modern organisations

Within organisations, employees typically fall into one of 4 categories:

Toxic	They are willfully destructive in the way they behave and the way they speak. They look to influence others on this path too.
Passive	They turn up and do the bare minimum, but aren't really interested in the company values and what the company is trying to achieve. They are self-interested at their core.
Active	They are actively involved within the organisation and buy into the purpose, the definition of the culture, the values and what the team or the organisation is looking to

	achieve. They want to work collectively with others to do this.
Drivers	And finally, they are a leading force for change within an organisation.

This relates to other concepts in team dynamics such as:

- Job-Career-Calling.
- Tuckman's 'Storming Forming Norming Performing' team model, a model which examines the way teams go through stages in their development.
- The 5-stage model within the book Tribal Leadership by Logan, King and Fischer-Wright. They describe 5 stages of *group behaviour*, going from a place of:
  - 'Life sucks'
  - 'Life sucks for me'
  - 'I'm great'
  - 'We're great'
  - 'Life is great'

In this model, it's believed the aim is to get people to the 'we're great' and then 'life is great' stages.

My model's Active and Driver Categories relate to the 3 models above in the following ways: a) People seeing their work as a calling, b) Performing stage, c) We're great and Life's Great stages.

Your primary goal as a leader is to work with everyone to move them to Active or Driver categories. Involve people in strategy, planning, culture and empower them to make changes. Trust them as a default and you will create a powerful collective.

What science tells us about the power of the collective

It's reassuring to see the power of the collective when we start to look at some of the science and research.

I saw an excellent wildlife series called Super/Natural in 2022. In one of the episodes, it showed a beehive being attacked by large hornets. To counter the attack, the bees collectively climbed on the hornets. They then raised their temperature to one they could sustain, but the hornet couldn't and they jointly burned the hornet alive! What an incredible example of the power of the collective, if somewhat brutal!

But the power and influence of groups has been found through time to be used in negative ways. Let's look at some key psychological research around *group behaviour* and initially go back to the 1950s.

In-group and out-group behaviour

In 1954 Muzafer Sherif carried out a famous piece of research called 'Robbers Cave', where he brought together 22 boys who had never met before. They were split into 2 groups and the introduction of competitive tasks led to overt hostility in a short space of time. It's interesting to note later co-operative tasks reduced conflict, highlighting again how shared goals can address group tensions. This was one of the founding pieces of research into in-group and out-group behaviour.

In-group and out-group behaviour is a form of cognitive bias and we're wired for this. We all tend to align with a group based on our survival instinct, and then see people who aren't part of the group as outsiders. We do this in part as a cognitive shortcut, because it's quicker and easier for us to identify people as either within our group or outside our group and this makes our processing of life simpler, which is what cognitive biases are there for. In-group and out-group behaviour may be understandable, but its consequences can be harmful and unfortunately it's at the root of prejudice.

Our need to conform

Another fascinating piece of psychological research was carried out by Solomon Asch in the 1950s. He got a group of people to decide whether a particular line drawn on a page matched with any one of 3 other lines. What Asch did in the experiment was to instruct all participants, apart from one person, to choose the wrong answer. The need for conformity led the lone ignorant participant to choose the wrong answer between 32% and 74% of the time! When questioned after, they admitted to being aware they were choosing the wrong answer. This demonstrates our compelling need to conform and be part of a group. Our *survival psychology* drives this basic need.

It's also fascinating we can conform to norms in particular situations as above, but in other situations this can then change and we don't feel the need to conform. To illustrate this let's go back to West Virginia at the time of segregation.

In 1952, Menard looked at black and white co-workers in West Virginia. At this time West Virginia was still very much impacted by laws of segregation between black and white people. Menard found when the workers were underground, there was conformity to norms in line with integrated worker relationships. But when they came back up, they went straight back to the ways of segregation. Conformity was seen to be situational.

A final piece of interesting psychological research in relation to conformity, was carried out by Zimbardo in 1971. Student volunteers entered a 2-week program and were assigned to either be prison guards or prisoners. In just a short period of time, the students so clearly identified with their role as guards and prisoners, there were acts of aggression and the students playing the roles of the prisoners requested to be removed from the experiment and it was terminated early.

Our need to conform will impact on our behaviour within and between groups and the area of obedience brings even more shocking insights into *group behaviour.*

Would we obey shocking instructions?

Let's examine a further piece of unsettling research from 1963 called 'Obedience to Authority', which in all honesty would not be conducted today due to its ethical issues. Psychologist Stanley Milgram (from Yale University) wanted to investigate the belief only certain groups of people would obey instructions to act in extremely hostile ways.

He recruited a group of volunteers to go into the experiment. They were put in a room with somebody who instructed them on what actions to take. The person instructing the participants was dressed to look official, wearing a white lab coat to increase the perceived level of authority. The participants were directed to ask someone in another room (an actor) a range of questions using radio mics. When people got questions wrong, they were told by the authority figure to administer increasingly large electrical shocks. Amazingly enough, this went right the way up to 450 volts! When the actors in the other room clearly showed signs of being in severe trauma and pain, 65% of the participants still continued with the shocks up to 450 volts.

As we can see, our potential to be obedient to authority figures is more likely to be universal. It was clearly a very unsettling piece of research, unethical and wouldn't be conducted in modern life, but the findings were startling. We may well end up doing things which would surprise or even shock us, due to our need to be accepted by leaders or authority figures. Leaders within organisations need to respect the power they have at their hands.

I've shared a range of fascinating and somewhat disturbing research into the power of the group and the power a leader can have over the group. We are wired to be part of groups, to lead and to follow. It's a key part of our evolutionary path and our *survival psychology*. We see this in all forms of society, including cults, revolutionary and terrorist groups.

The intertwining of ourselves and the social context is seen through many psychological theories including social constructionist, social learning theory and observational learning. We are intrinsically social beings and this goes right back to the origins of our species. We are social and we also seek out leadership.

Leadership and evolution

In Mark van Vugt's book 'Selected', he put forward the concept of 'Evolutionary Leadership Theory' where leading and following are seen as a set of adaptive behavioural strategies which have evolved over time to solve social coordination problems and to keep us safe. The relationship between leaders and followers is key to this. Unfortunately, as we've seen in the chapter on *ego*, leaders can abuse their position of power for their own benefit or at the expense of others.

But it can also be used as a force for good. When we function at our best, we can make incredible changes working as a collective. This includes major communities working together during catastrophes, space exploration, Live Aid and creating the World Wide Web. None of these feats were achieved by an individual, they were achieved by a collective. Organisations can utilise *group behaviour* as a force for good in the way the culture is developed too.

Positive organisational culture

Organisations which build a culture around a common purpose, an aspirational vision, shared values, behaviour and language, can move mountains. When the right people are on board (Active or Drivers in the earlier model), aligned with the culture and empowered to take things forward, this is when an organisation and its people is at its best.

As Peter Drucker once said: "Culture eats strategy for breakfast". More importantly it comes before strategy. If the culture is wrong, strategy will be incredibly hard to develop and implement. Culture will be the foundation for organisational *group behaviour.*

Organisational group behaviour

You can see examples of unified groups within many organisations like Apple. For many years Apple has had a philosophy of simplicity. You can see this in the product design and packaging. It also runs through the way they hold meetings (keeping the number of people in meetings to a bare minimum and the meetings short) and their approach to marketing. Keeping it simple is a philosophy which has pervaded right the way through Apple. It built a loyal group within the organisation and this extended to its customers.

You often see unification around an agreed culture done in brilliant ways within organisations and teams, where people are aligned behind a set of values, behaviours and purpose.

When I've flown with both Emirates and Jet2, there is a consistency of behaviour and alignment which their people appear to authentically buy into. I always remember one situation when I turned up early for a flight coming back from Dubai, where I'd been working. The flight attendant (on the check-in desk) said "I see you're early and we have availability on a flight which is going slightly earlier than your flight. Would this be better for you?" And with no fuss she made all this happen. My experience on that occasion is very indicative of the behaviour I see by all Emirates staff.

A US company called IDEO 101 strives to do the right things to convince their group of people that new recruits are right for the company. One of the actions is to take potential new recruits out to lunch with ten current employees to get their thoughts! This is true involvement.

Examples of strong *group behaviour* can be seen in various aspects of life, particularly in sport.

Lessons from sport

In 2022, Brendon 'Baz' McCullum was appointed coach and Ben Stokes captain of the England cricket team. They've developed a concept called 'Bazball', where the team unified around a collective mindset in which they're freer to make mistakes so they learn and grow. Additionally, they focus on taking wickets rather than the runs scored by the opposition, batters express themselves rather than feel fearful and fielding positions are less defensive. This has all made for a culture which puts entertaining first, rather than being fearful of losing. This is a clear purpose of 'Bazball'.

In the book Legacy, James Kerr took an in depth look at the All Blacks rugby team (the most successful sports team in history). Their culture hit a period where it had become toxic, with too much partying and little pride in wearing the team shirt. Work was done to rebuild the culture, with a strong sense of purpose and unity. They would share the history of the team via a 'Black Book', the team would work collectively to support each other and there was a ritual when people were first given the shirt to wear at the start of their international career. This returned the team to a high-performance culture.

It's worth noting the All Blacks have recently hit a period of poor performance (including their biggest loss in history to the Springboks in 2023) and this is believed to be partly down to a new leader and loss of focus on some of the core values of the past. We can build great group cultures, but we can lose them too.

The mind-traps leaders face with group behaviour

Group behaviour can be an empowering force for leaders, but it can also undermine leaders and teams. Here are some examples:

- A feeling of disconnect between the shopfloor and office staff damaging morale and impacting performance
- Struggling with the isolation of working from home and missing the social connection
- An 'us and them' culture where management aren't trusted to share important information with employees in the organisation
- Toxic individuals forming breakaway groups and using WhatsApp to undermine the leader
- Many examples of individuals being discriminated against or treated inappropriately due to gender, sexual identity, race or disability

These are just a small sample of the more detrimental impacts of *group behaviour* and the need to form groups. You will certainly have your own stories and examples.

Let's look at some of the challenges which can be faced in relation to *group behaviour* in more detail. They can range from all the forms of discrimination I've highlighted within society and organisations, right the way through to the impact on somebody standing in front of a group of people to present!

Cognitive biases

We need to be aware of biases which impact leaders and teams. Firstly, the tendency to be drawn towards an in-group and be hostile to an out-group (as was visibly demonstrated by the experiment of Sheriff). This can be seen in organisations with silo behaviour, 'us and them' cultures and discrimination.

We also see biases in 'Cognitive Ancestral Leader Prototypes' (from the work of Mark van Vugt) where in times of risk and conflict people are drawn to younger masculine individuals as leaders (this is also known as the Big Man theory or Great Man Theory). It's one of the root causes why there still aren't anywhere near enough women in senior leadership positions around the world.

We are more complex in our thinking in modern life, but still undermined by primitive group thinking and functioning. Leaders and individuals need to raise their awareness of how these and other biases can play out in organisations, to handle the negative impact.

Discrimination in all its forms

As described the bias relating to in-group alignment directly influences various forms of discrimination: racism, ableism, transphobia, homophobia, misogyny. All of these impact the world in a wider sense, but they can also impact your organisations. It's crucial to stamp this out and work on this to enable a diverse, inclusive and connected workforce.

However small you are, you need to look at EDIB (Equality Diversity Inclusivity Belonging) procedures and policies. As a leader you need to model the right behaviour and ensure you and others call out discriminatory behaviour in any area of the organisation.

Another key divider of people is the feeling there is a divide between management and employees or office and shopfloor staff.

Us and them cultures

Within organisations, people can fall into 'us and them' positions, particularly where they feel management aren't on their side, don't share information or aren't to be trusted. An 'us and them' divide is fear based and can eat away at trust to ultimately damage relationships and performance. It can also occur where there is a lack of connection between shop floor or manual workers and office staff. We are social beings and if we are disconnected it damages relationships critical to the results we're looking to achieve.

Disconnection within organisations is also not helped by the disparity of rewards. The ratio of CEO pay to the lowliest paid workers is over 100 times higher in US and UK companies. Is your organisation rewarding fairly?

There are further ways in which people can feel divided, which can be damaging for culture and performances.

Silos forming in organisations

Silo behaviour can be rife in organisations. Teams blaming and criticising other teams, not sharing information or seeing knowledge as power. Destructive forms of competition can be promoted by leaders or happen as a matter of course. You can also find cliques form within organisations and teams which can leave others feeling ostracised. Silo thinking can create small groups which kill wider connection.

Building a culture which breaks this down and unifies everyone around the common purpose, aspirations and values is critical to stamping out silo behaviour. The culture needs to be monitored and picked up at every point in the working day.

The impact of mergers

A spin-off example of silos is when one or more companies are brought together in a merger. Often this means bringing together different cultures and values and it's why due diligence is so important beforehand, to ensure there is reasonable alignment in purpose, values and behaviours.

A merger needs careful managing throughout with open communication and allowing people on all sides to have a voice. People on both sides will be fearful of the changes which may occur and what it may mean for them and the *survival psychology* will be on high alert!

I've seen companies make decisions not to go ahead with acquisitions, when there is clear value misalignment and this is a wise move to take.

The dangers of groupthink

We looked at the research behind the human need to conform and obey. Groupthink is a phenomenon which occurs when a group of individuals reaches a consensus without critical reasoning or evaluation of the consequences or alternatives. Groupthink is based on a common desire not to upset the balance of a group of people.

As a leader it's important to put your *ego* to one side and ensure you are not encouraging groupthink within your teams. Your people need to be able to think freely, challenge and put forward different ideas. Your culture needs to be strong and secure and provide the psychological safety to counter the tendency towards groupthink.

The damage done by toxic individuals and groups

Toxic individuals may be a small minority in an organisation, but they can create toxic groups leading to toxic cultures. Disenfranchised individuals (the first of my 4-category model earlier) can influence the creation of toxic breakaway groups who seek to undermine leaders and teams.

I've seen this in organisations where secret WhatsApp groups and other social media groups are formed, with the intention of bad-mouthing leaders and companies. A toxic individual can ultimately become an influential toxic group and this can even lead to criminal activity.

Your organisation or your team will develop a culture by default. If you don't proactively do something about it, then it will cause you problems.

The fear of public speaking based on group behaviour

Another interesting challenge you may face as a leader, which has some of its origins in our need to belong to groups, is the fear of public speaking or as it's known more officially 'Glossophobia'. Surprisingly, this is a fear found in many surveys to be more prominent and worse than the fear of flying, spiders or even the fear of death!

It's interesting to understand the root causes of this fear as, in my experience, it's 2-fold.

Firstly, when we stand in front of a group, the more primitive parts of our brain don't connect with or understand the complexity of modern life. There is part of your psyche which sees a group of people in the room as being a danger. Part of your psyche will be telling you to get out of the room for your own safety, it will feel threatened. It doesn't understand the difference between being back thousands or millions of years ago fighting for physical survival, or being in front of a group of business people you're just about to deliver a presentation to.

Secondly, when you stand in front of a group of people, your anxiety and nerves will build because you fear you may be ostracised from the group in front of you. The fear is especially raised if it's a group of peers. Speaking to many leaders over time, I've found they're particularly nervous presenting to people who are in their own industry. The fear of being found out and disconnected from the group is triggering your need for group unity and to belong.

The future of leadership and organisations

With our moves to more remote and hybrid working, group relationships will continue to adapt and change in the future. I have many conversations with leaders about their needs versus those of their people on this front. We all need to acknowledge that the demands of 'Generation Z' and 'Generation Alpha' will further us along this path.

It's more important to focus on the quality of the culture, the relationships and the way people communicate in all its forms. Your ways of working will need attention, whether your people work solely in the office, fully remotely in a hybrid form. Don't fixate on the tools and channels of communication and work locations, focus on the quality of relationships. The real power of groups has nothing to do with tools and everything to do with people, relationships and how they interact.

How to escape the mind-traps of group behaviour

* Mindset

We must acknowledge everyone's need for connection. We need to be part of groups and it's important to understand how this impacts us in all forms of life, whether it's playing in a sports team or groups which are a strong part of our personal identity (such as our gender identity, our race and sexual orientation).

We need to be much more mindful and aware of how group behaviour can impact us individually and how it can influence others. Awareness always gives us greater power. It takes us to a place where we can 'understand the fear' first before acting. Know group behaviour can be a force for bad and cause problems. But it can also be an incredible force for good.

Your psychological safety requires focus for you as an individual. Psychological safety also needs to be at the forefront of your mind in the culture you lead for your people. Know psychological safety will be very much undermined by some of the examples of group behaviour we've been speaking about. Have a zero-tolerance mindset for the negative impacts of discrimination, silo and toxic behaviour.

* Practical tools and actions for you

Here are a number of practical tools and actions which will support you in relation to *group behaviour*. Select the 1 or 2 you feel addresses your biggest challenges and focus on these first.

a) Work on your culture

As I stated at the beginning of this chapter, your company or your team will be as strong as the culture you have established for your people. A culture will exist, whether you work on it or not, so being intentional in creating this is the way forward.

Involve all your people in co-creating the culture, as this is the best way to ensure it is both right and adhered to. To get your people to the stage where they're 'Active' and hopefully even 'Drivers' within your culture, you'll need them to be fully involved. They will want to feel like they have power in shaping the future of the organisation. Don't lapse into a culture of conformity, where people feel unable to challenge and bring new ideas. It is the relationship of individuals with others and their environment which will drive culture and so this needs to be done holistically.

Defining your culture will predominantly be derived from the core components which have existed for many years:

- Look at the purpose and meaning of your organisation. A shared purpose will create unstoppable energy. What are you about?

- What is your vision? What are you looking to achieve for society in a wider perspective that will be your legacy?

- What values will you have in place which everybody knows and will guide behaviour?

- Then what behaviours will ensure you demonstrate your values consistently, inside and outside the organisation? It could also be you have identified language, words or phrases people all connect with and which are of common parlance. It isn't just about setting values, it's about living values!

- Get your people playing to their strengths too and working in areas which interest them as much as possible

If you look to acquire or merge with other organisations, it is important to do the due diligence on financials and organisational governance. But it's critical to do this for the cultures, to ensure you are aligned as this can often be the biggest hurdle.

b) Lead ethically

As a leader you are entrusted with a great degree of power. There is much good which can be done with this as we've seen. But we've also seen the many ways leading groups of people can go significantly wrong. This book will raise your awareness of areas to be mindful of:

- Discrimination in all its forms
- In-group and out-group behaviour
- Silo behaviour, 'us and them' cultures
- People's tendency to conform and obey when part of a group
- The cognitive biases which can play out in people's minds

Your responsibility is to continue to learn more and to lead people ethically and with care.

c) Positivity will build connection and unity

As you saw in the chapter on *defensive mindset,* Psychologist Marcial Losada found the ratio of positive feedback to more critical feedback should be at least 3:1 for high performing teams (known as 'The Losada Line'). Find opportunities to congratulate and appreciate your people – individually and collectively.

Share stories of great achievements and milestones regularly and these can be built into a 'Black Book' as the All Blacks did, which you can share physically or online with potential new recruits.

I worked with a CEO of an Educational Trust who did this very thing, by collating excellent case studies to build into a book to share with parents, new recruits and students.

d) Look at how you collaborate within your organisation

An Individual's *ego* needs to be surrendered to the collective good (we examined the damage done by *ego* in the previous chapter). Your aim is to get people to collaborate and use their collective intelligence. Leadership and power must be distributed throughout your organisation. Enable people to co-create solutions and ways forward.

The book 'Leadership Is Language' by L. David Marquet (retired US Navy Captain) looks at the loss of a ship and highlights the inadequacies of 'Industrial Age' style leadership in the complex modern world. The ship was lost due to the unwillingness of the captain to take on board the collective intelligence of others on-board. Marquet defines workers as either 'red or blue workers' (team members or leaders) and highlights how important it is to have the red workers, the people who aren't in management positions, very much bringing their expertise and knowledge to the changes and decisions needing to be made.

Know one plus one will always be greater than two or, looking at it in a different way from 'gestalt psychology', the whole will always be greater than the sum of its parts!

e) As a senior leader your loyalty is to your senior team first

As a leader you need to take on board the views of your team and represent them at a senior level, but the group you need to show loyalty to first is the senior team. If trust breaks down at this level, it will be corrosive.

Yes, you need to be loyal to your team and members and represent their views. But your primary loyalty is to the senior team and the collective decision making therein.

This is explored very well in the book 'The 5 Dysfunctions of a Team' by Patrick Lencioni.

f) Deal with toxic individuals and isolate them

If there are people undermining leaders and teams, you ignore this at your peril. First see if you can do anything with them to adapt and change their behaviour. To address their issues and bring them on side. If not, move swiftly following a performance management process (with HR guidance) to remove them from the organisation. I've seen far too many organisations tolerate destructive individuals for too long. Don't shy away from acting to deal with toxic individuals, as a toxic individual can influence the formation of a toxic group and this will become a much bigger problem.

g) Flex your leadership style to suit the person and situation

You will need to be more directive at times (especially at times of crisis or emergency). At other times, you need to be more democratic. There will be situations where you need to coach or support people. It may be they need you to be more attuned to their emotional needs, to deal with personal problems.

Be able to adapt and flex your leadership style, to bring unity and get the best out of your individuals. Getting the best out of your people (and yourself) also needs you to delegate and release more of your responsibilities.

If adapting your leadership style is an area of interest, it is covered excellently in Daniel Goleman's book 'The New Leaders'.

h) Overcommunicate

Your teams will be helped by the way you communicate and the amount of information you share. I would encourage you to push yourself out of your comfort zone and share more and more information with your people. Don't protect information, even though there may be certain downsides you need to take on board and prepare for. The more you show trust and share information, the more you'll build a unified team or organisation.

Use a range of channels – face to face, meetings, newsletters, intranets, email, calls – and know that important messages may need repetition to ensure they are clear and understood.

Communication and engagement will have the effect of tightening the links within the group. Communication also requires listening. Be ready to listen to opinions and ideas at all levels and be prepared to act or empower your people to act on them.

i) Understand the inner world of other people

As a leader, you can build much stronger teams by demonstrating empathy, and theory of mind.

Be ready to understand what is going on in other people's worlds, how they're thinking and why they're thinking in this way (theory of mind). Also dig deeper to discover how they feel about changes (empathy).

Be prepared to show some vulnerability (as we covered in the chapter on *ego)* so they can show their vulnerability too.

j) Endeavour to keep your groups small

Ideally keep things small. Whether it's Dunbar's number of 150 people or 520 from more recent research, know the primitive parts of your people's brains will have limitations in the relationships which can be meaningfully formed. The more organisations grow, the more bureaucracy increases and it becomes harder to build unity, so push against this continually. Break things down into satellites, whilst also keeping bridges across those satellites.

k) Build strong teams which work together across silos

Work to ensure your teams are co-operating together rather than competing. Break down barriers between shopfloor and office staff. Communication will also be key to helping management and employees having an open trusting relationship.

Shared values will have a strong influence on breaking down these barriers and one or 2 values focused on collaboration and co-operation can support this.

Align people behind broader cohesive goals which will pull teams together to achieve those collectively.

l) HR practices, procedures and policies

Whatever the size of your organisation, when you employ people you need to have EDIB (Equality Diversity Inclusivity Belonging) procedures and policies in place (along with broader HR policies) to ensure an inclusive and diverse workforce. There needs to be zero tolerance for issues relating to racism, ableism, transphobia, homophobia, misogyny or any discrimination within your organisation or team.

Some discrimination will be entrenched or structural and it may need deeper work doing, but commit to making the changes as speedily as possible.

It's good for us to be connected within organisations, but we also need to respect everybody's differences and their uniqueness.

m) Office, remote and hybrid working

As discussed earlier, we need to be very mindful of what the future of work looks like. Hybrid and remote working can be good for individuals, with benefits for their life outside work. It can benefit organisations, with less or no office space needed. It can also cause big problems when there is a lack of connection.

Talk to your people, be open and find ways which are going to work for them as individuals and for your teams and organisation. Be mindful that although people may feel it's in their best interest as individuals to work from home, the long-term issues for mental health from being isolated can be problematic. We are at our core social creatures.

I work with a number of organisations who still have remote or hybrid working in place post pandemic. They still periodically review this and check in with their people to be confident this is still for the best.

Get the culture, level of leadership support and communication right whichever route you take.

n) Mind your language

Within teams and organisations look at the language used consistently. Does this support the culture as I touched on in the first point? Unify people with certain words and phrases which will support the culture. Pick up on group language which is unhelpful – 'us and them', competitive language, put downs of other teams and such like. Language will determine behaviour. Even a simple shift from 'I' to 'We' can have a big impact, as we saw looking at the issues around *ego*.

You may have heard of the research of Alvert Mehrabian, which has been widely misused. It's used to suggest only 7% of communication is down to words, but this is considerably higher.

o) Present with a clear perspective and a growth mindset

Knowing and being aware of what is going on when we stand up to present or speak in public will give us a sense of perspective, which we can then rationalise more easily.

I once had a client who rang me on the day of her event in a panic. We talked about the fact nobody was going to die, her business would not be destroyed and she reached a place of calm.

Speaking is important, but not as critical as our *survival psychology* may have us believe! Approach any event with a growth mindset. You won't be perfect, but you can take feedback and reflect to enable you to grow and improve.

p) Nudge your groups into change

Nudging is an interesting strategy to influence changes in behaviour for groups of people. Rather than directing, you influence in more subtle ways.

The most bizarre example of this was a psychologist painting a small fly on men's urinals to get them to aim at it and improve their aim and the hygiene of the toilets!

q) Use triads

When I worked at Experian as a senior leader in the early 2000s, I was put in a leadership trio with 2 other leaders. We shared challenges, experience and knowledge and it was incredibly useful and supportive. This was my first experience of the power of 3.

Many relationships are 121 in organisations. Managers are often likely to communicate in dyadic ways with others. Linking people and teams together to solve problems collectively can be a great way to break down silos, use combined intelligence and build relationships. As a senior leader, are you communicating independently with other leaders, when bringing them together would bring greater impact?

r) Step up and lead

Leadership does not need to come through a title. We can all lead. If you believe in something passionately, find other people who will support you in the cause. It can be within organisations or in life in general.

All of the following stood up and led groups to make big changes in our lives - Nelson Mandela, Rosa Parks, Emmeline Pankhurst, Bod Geldof, Mark Zuckerberg.

Summary

- Know that we are still, at our core, driven by *group behaviour.* Our need to be part of a group goes back right to the origins of the Homo species 2 million years ago. It is fear based and seen as key to our survival

- People want to be part of groups and will look for leaders and leadership. The need for this puts a responsibility on leaders to act in a way that has integrity, trust and authenticity

- Through all the research I've shared on conformity, obedience and in-group and out-group behaviour, know that group unity can be a force for good and it can be a force for bad. It's our collective responsibility to use *group behaviour* as a force for good and deal with the more negative aspects such as discrimination, silo behaviour, us and them cultures or toxic behaviour

- Through our awareness of some of the more undermining aspects of *group behaviour* and by focusing on the good things that we can do to unify people behind a cause, we can use *group behaviour* as a significant power for good!

We have examined 4 out of the 5 parts of my *survival psychology* model. We now finally turn to *negative self-talk,* an area which feeds all the other 4 mind-traps of *survival psychology.*

5. NEGATIVE SELF-TALK

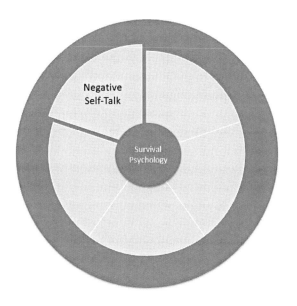

"We are continually thinking and often our thoughts are more doubtful or negative in nature, but we have the superpower to shift them."

How many thoughts do you think we have every single day?

We are plagued by 1000s of ANTs every day. Not the insects you have running in out of your house during the summer months, but 'Automatic Negative Thoughts'. We are continually thinking and the majority of this is unconscious; much of it is both doubtful and negative in nature (80% of our thoughts are negative according to the National Science Foundation).

In past research it was believed we had around 50-60,000 thoughts every day. I've seen more recent research where it was found human beings typically have over 6,000 thoughts every day (Tseng and Poppenk - using MRI scans with 184 participants).

In Eckhart Tolle's book 'New Earth', he describes a story where he noticed a woman on the underground talking to herself incessantly in a loud and angry voice. He got off the tube at the same stop as her, as she continually spoke out loud with no break in the stream of words. She entered a University of London building and Tolle had time to reflect. How could an apparently insane person like her be part of the University? He thought, I hope I don't end up like her, but then he realised he'd mumbled those words aloud. He was already like her! He realised his mind was as active as hers and if she was mad, everyone was mad, including himself.

As a leader your *negative self-talk* can be incessant, frequently trip you up and hijack you, sapping your confidence and making you indecisive. It can hold you back and impact on your happiness and fulfilment and this is why it's vital to understand what's going on to enable you to manage it.

It starts with evolution.

Wiring to keep us safe

Thinking in more doubtful or negative ways is fear based and it's normal. It is primarily about keeping us safe. As discussed before, our prehistoric ancestors survived by constantly being on the lookout for threats and dangers, fixing problems as they were encountered. The adversity they feared was mostly physical in nature.

In modern life, we still scan our environments for threats and dangers, but we turn this inwards and start to look for our own weaknesses and vulnerabilities. We look for threats to our self-esteem and the practicalities of our lives. Our fears are more psychological in nature.

Imagination is one of the best qualities of the human mind and we can use it to imagine potential threats and assess our ability to handle them. Doing this enables us to solve problems before we get into trouble, but this capability to imagine threats can also work against us as we become fixated with imagining all sorts of impending disasters and failings on our part.

Our *survival psychology* will continually exaggerate, distort and imagine threats which can hijack us and block our creativity and potential. It can quickly put us into fight, flight or freeze mode. Survival thinking results in a biased view of world in front of us. In modern life, we have become too uncomfortable with discomfort. Often perceived adversity is just something which will cause us discomfort. It's not life threatening or even especially significant for the most part.

The negativity bias

The *negative self-talk* emanating from our *survival psychology* can become habitual if we're not careful. According to the research of Dr Fred Luskin of Stanford University, 90% of our ANTs are repetitive. Repeated negative thinking will over time develop neural pathways of negativity!

Repeated negative thinking can leave us with what is known as a negativity bias in our thinking, where we tend to register and dwell on negative stimuli and events more readily. The negativity bias means we feel the sting of things which go wrong more powerfully than we feel the joy. This can feed into the perpetuating feeling of 'not being good enough'. It also explains to a degree why first impressions can be difficult to overcome and why difficult and negative events have more of a long lingering effect on us. This can play out in the workplace with projects that go wrong, mistakes made by people, challenges with customers. There's always good and bad happening on a daily basis, it's a matter of what we focus on as a leader and what we give emphasis to.

As human beings, we tend to remember traumatic experiences better than positive ones, recall insults better than praise and react more strongly to negative stimuli. We think about negative things more frequently than positives. As I indicated earlier, we can spend up to 80% of our time thinking negatively out of the 1,000s of daily thoughts. Our *survival psychology* wants to keep us safe so it's repeatedly on the lookout for potential problems and pitfalls and this can lead us to focus on the potential bad.

Famous psychologist Barbara Fredrickson carried out research where she got a number of participants on a daily basis to tally the number of positive emotions they experienced against the number of negative ones. She found the bad was considerably higher than good.

The media tap into this tendency in a very big way. We find the newspapers and TV news are preoccupied with tales of catastrophe and problems in the world. They understand only too well our tendency to get drawn to the negative. In fact, it's been found in studies that negative news is also more likely to be believed as truthful. Negative information prompts greater attention and it also may be seen as having greater validity. As leaders, we can be greatly influenced by the bigger issues playing out in the world, when in reality we may have little control over them and they may not impact us as much as we believe.

Our *survival psychology* is very much at play here. Survival thinking will get triggered if there's any potential danger. Often the danger in the newspapers is not directly threatening to us, but our *survival psychology* has difficulty in interpreting this correctly. It can vastly exaggerate threats and lead to poor decision making, as we grapple with a significant inner battle.

I clearly remember the recession of 2008, where the media fed the fear of this, leading to many poor, short sighted decisions by heads of companies from a place of fear.

The inner battle between the potential self and the destructive self

Our biggest battle as leaders is the internal battle between our *potential self*, the amazing potential we're born with, and our *destructive self*. The destructive side of our psyche is very much driven by our *Survival Psychology,* with the pessimism and anxiety triggered by it.

We all exist on a spectrum in relation to our *potential self* and *destructive self*. From day to day, moment to moment, we can find ourselves moving from one end of the spectrum to the other. You may start the day feeling incredibly upbeat about the day ahead, only to go out and find your car tyre is flat. Then a further sequence of events can lead you to get hooked by your 'destructive self' quite speedily.

The level of problematic thinking humans encounter has been a direct influence on why psychology became preoccupied with problems of the mind over the years (a ratio of 17:1 in terms of research into negative aspects and disorders with the mind versus positive and enabling research). It took Martin Seligman in 1995, to move the psychology movement to look more at how the mind can be used to serve us rather than focusing only on merely identifying psychological problems and various forms of mental illness.

Throughout this chapter, I'm going to be looking at the concept of *negative self-talk* and how it can present challenges for you as a leader. There is much to get to grips with here, but a greater understanding of what is going on will lead you to have greater control of your 'destructive self'. As with the other chapters, in the latter part of this chapter I'm going to share ways you can move forward and engage your 'potential self' to fulfil much more of your potential. We need to 'understand the fear first', as *negative self-talk* is fear-based.

Understanding negative self-talk

We've looked at 4 areas of my *survival psychology* model so far. They are interrelated and all relate directly with the area of *negative self-talk*. *Impostor syndrome, defensive mindset, ego* and *group behaviour* all involve *negative self-talk* in the way they play out. Handling *negative self-talk* is an all-encompassing challenge.

Understanding the biological basis of *negative self-talk* will help you recognise it's not a personal failing of yours, but is influenced by human nature, survival thinking and your brain chemistry. Through this, you will be able to gain greater control of yourself as you develop as a leader.

We are born with default wiring to be pessimistic. According to Dr Martin Seligman "What got selected for in the Ice Ages, was 'bad weather animals', who were always thinking about the awful stuff that could occur. As a result of this, what comes naturally to people is pessimism".

Our outlook can also be impacted over time, through life's experiences and relationships. Much of this is stored within our unconscious mind, which is a driver of those 'automatic negative thoughts' described earlier.

With *negative self-talk* as a large part of those 1000s of thoughts we have every day, we can be gripped by an inner monologue. We have thoughts and we believe they must be part of our identity and we follow them down rabbit holes and they can become self-fulfilling prophecies. We own them as part of our identity. They reinforce the default human position of 'not being good enough'.

The concept of having a negative mindset, emotions and thoughts has been covered throughout time. Whether it be Freud and the emotional drives from the 'id', Dr Steve Peters and the emotional 'chimp' or Eckhart Tolle and his view of the 'pain body'. All these concepts focus on the emotionally driven part of our personality, which in reality we do not have to own or be a victim of in the way we typically are. It's survival orientated, fear based and very often misguided.

The neurology of fear

We need to be mindful of how we react to potential threats. Jospeh LeDoux calls this the 'quick and dirty route'. When we react to potential danger, there's a direct route through to the amygdala (the emotional part of the brain), which then triggers a number of reactions in the body:

- Blood pressure increases
- Cortisol and adrenaline are released
- Our field of vision can be narrowed
- Brain frequency increases

It's important to note that a higher brain frequency (12 Hz and above) stifles our creativity and our ability to problem solve in a positive way.

The alternative route is where the cerebral cortex (the rational thinking part of the brain) is engaged to process the threat more logically. Information takes both paths, but the problem is that it moves more speedily through the 'quick and dirty route' to engage the emotional part of our brain and our fight or flight response. We react speedily to fear and perceived adversity. Reacting in this way can tip the balance between pessimism and optimism and make us more focused on threats and potential adversity.

Pessimism and optimism

I stated earlier we're very much wired for pessimism, but we also have the innate ability to develop our optimistic thinking and outlook. We can continually rewire our neurology and one of the most important ways we can do this is by shifting our mindset, thinking and perspective from a more pessimistic view to a more optimistic view.

There are 4 main ways in which we can get fixated with a pessimistic mindset when things go wrong (informed by the 'explanatory styles' of Martin Seligman, the father of positive psychology movement):

1. We believe a negative event will continue through time and won't just be a short-lived event we can move on from.

2. We also believe it doesn't just affect one aspect of our life or work, it can expand its reach to impact on other areas unnecessarily. When this happens, it can be particularly dangerous for leaders if they are experiencing problems at work, and it starts to affect their personal life or vice versa.

3. The third aspect of having a more pessimistic outlook is when we believe it's all our fault. We don't take account of the external factors which may have brought about the problem and totally blame ourselves.

4. Finally, a pessimistic view will hold if there's nothing that can be done by us to get ourselves out of a particular challenge. This relates to the concept called 'Learned Helplessness' explained further on in the chapter.

When we consistently get drawn into those 4 areas of pessimistic thinking and *negative self-talk* it can cause deep rooted problems, leading to mental health challenges and depression.

This was my journey in late 2012, which ended up with me being diagnosed with depression and it was a journey of 6 months plus to get me back to a stronger place with my mental health. My work is focused on ensuring others don't end up in this place too.

The more we can move to an optimistic position in those 4 areas, the more self-empowering this will be. Being optimistic is when:

1. We see problems as being just short lived.
2. We compartmentalise them and don't let them affect other parts of our lives or work.
3. We see the external factors impacting on why things went wrong.
4. We believe we can do something about it.

Optimism is very much tied to our level of happiness and fulfilment in leadership positions.

Our level of happiness

In Shaun Achor's book 'Happiness Advantage', he suggested we mostly live our lives by an equation which is the wrong way around. We believe when we achieve a level of success, then we'll be happy. But a vast amount of research (200 studies covering 275,000 people) shows it's actually by focusing on happiness that we will become more successful.

Research (from Lyubomirsky in 2005) has also shown 40% of the variation in our happiness is within our control (10% more circumstantial and 50% genes and biology), which gives us all a positive view on our ability to shape our own happiness and in turn our success.

Included within the factors which influence our happiness is our level of optimism. The more we can influence our self-talk and level of optimism in positive ways, it will lead us to be happier and fulfilled and will result in greater success (as we've been discussing throughout).

Being more optimistic can be trained as a habit. The 'Tetris Effect' is a phenomenon where, due to continually playing the game Tetris (a game where groups of squares are moved to fit into a building pattern), people see other aspects of life based on square patterns. For example, visualising buildings moving positions to fit into gaps in the horizon etc. If we can be trained to look for patterns based on a simple game, we can be trained to look for patterns in life. Seeing positive patterns in our life and work is helped by consciously recording good things about every day (as we will examine further in the solutions section). It will not only help to recognise results, but it will also have an impact on them too.

Thinking impacts results

Our thinking will very much influence the results we achieve in our leadership role. It can shift us from pessimism to optimism and can increase our levels of happiness and fulfilment. All this improves the results we achieve.

There was a fascinating piece of research done with GPs (from Shaun Achor), where it was found when GPs were encouraged into a more positive frame of mind, they improved the speed and accuracy of diagnosis by 19%. How did they put GPs in a more positive frame of mind? With the promise of sweets! Not even giving them sweets, because that would have affected their blood sugar levels and may have been a confounding variable in the research. But just the promise of sweets put them in a better frame of mind with the result they were more effective in their role.

Your thinking will directly influence your performance as a leader.

I've been working with leaders via my company since 2007 and I call myself a 'Leadership Psychologist' because, a) this is my qualification and b) I passionately believe leaders' number one challenge is their own internal thinking and mindset. This is very much impacted by the mind-traps of *survival psychology* and can play out in the negative monologue which damages confidence, self-belief, identity and ultimately performance.

A big problem is, if we allow our *negative self-talk* to have a driving power in our relationship with self, it can lead not only to a loss of confidence, but to a position where we feel we're unable to do anything about the problems we face. Martin Seligman conceptualised this as 'Learned Helplessness', where we cease trying because we believe the results will always be negative and unchangeable. As a leader this can be extremely destructive and you may well become disempowered by a feeling of continually hitting a brick wall or being dis-empowered to make the changes needed.

Perspectives change physical outcomes

Your thinking will influence not only your view of self, but your view of the world and your experiences. Take for example the difference between what are called a 'nocebo effect' and 'placebo effect'. It's been found when patients have a more negative view about the treatment they're about to receive, the treatment can have a more negative effect than it would otherwise have had. For example, if patients anticipate side effects from medication, they can experience them even if the medication is an inert substance! This is the 'nocebo effect' in action. The opposite of this is the 'placebo effect', where positive expectations can lead to improved outcomes from medication (again even if inert).

Our minds and beliefs are incredibly powerful. Japanese researchers blindfolded 13 students and told them poison ivy was being rubbed on their arm. All 13 students broke out in hives and a rash on that arm. The thing is they were only being rubbed with a harmless leaf. Their skin reacted to what they believed was happening. In another scenario, students were told a harmless plant was being rubbed on their other arm although it actually was poison ivy. Only 2 of the 13 students broke out in hives and a rash on that arm.

As leaders, we can shift our perspectives and those of others to become more enabling. Our individual and collective thinking will directly change results. The words we use will play a key role in changing our thinking and perspectives.

Words have power

Words play a significant part in communicating with others, but importantly when communicating with ourselves. The more we're conscious and pick ourselves up when we're using more doubtful or negative words and change them to positive, it will influence our mindset, beliefs, and the results we achieve. It's also especially notable that we use words to label and describe self. The key words or phrases we use either empower us and feed our 'potential self' or disempower us by feeding the 'destructive self'.

Some example words and expressions to be mindful of are:

- "I can't", "I'm not able" and other expressions which limit ourselves
- "Massive", "Huge" and other exaggerated expressions
- "Terrible", "Impossible" and other emotive words of this nature
- "But" which negates what was said before. "I did well on that, but…"
- "Try", "Might", "Possibly" amongst a collection of doubtful words

I once worked with a leader who said "I might try and do that" when we were talking about a potential action for him. I made him aware I'd never heard a less certain proclamation in my work! The negative and doubtful words we use can be an indication of how we're thinking and feeling. They can also influence how we think and feel too.

Daily communication with our people also involves listening to them in the right way. Our 'destructive self' can impact on how we receive the words of others.

Listening filters to be mindful of

In your role as a leader, be mindful of the way you listen to people and how your *negative self-talk* can hijack this. Being present for people can be difficult when your survival thinking kicks in and wants to decipher what problem needs fixing or, even worse, whether they think you're responsible for a problem. Your survival thinking may also be fixated on another issue separate to this discussion.

Your *negative self-talk* can take over and hamper your ability to be present and pay attention. A greater focus on consciously listening and not being drawn to your inner conversations will help here.

Listening to positive feedback on your performance and giving appreciative feedback to others in your teams also needs you to be more mindful.

Receiving and giving positive feedback

Be mindful of the *negative self-talk* which may well hijack the receiving of positive praise and feedback from your people on your leadership. Know praise can be dismissed quickly, deferred to others, reflected back or the impact downplayed.

Take positive praise without questioning and give praise as sincerely and specifically as possible to counter the *negative self-talk* in others. Don't just praise in passing but spend quality time explaining why this was a good piece of work.

I've seen far too many examples of a "well done" being shared, without expanding on this, with the result that it does not land with any lasting impact for the person receiving it.

Many of the pitfalls we have been examining in this chapter will become a heightened problem if we're not conscious. Let's explore this area further.

Consciousness in humans

The area of consciousness is a very important one for us to cover in relation to *negative self-talk*. I have used the word 'conscious' on a number of occasions. As a leader you will often drop into autopilot or unconscious thinking and behaviour.

Neuroscientist Joseph LeDoux examined consciousness in his book 'Anxious'. He noted that, while animals (particularly mammals), may have emotional responses to events, humans have the added capacity for higher order cognitive processing and self-awareness. As humans, we can bring conscious awareness to our emotional states in a more elaborate manner than animals. Our ability to do this gives us incredible power and conscious self-awareness enables us to articulate and analyse our emotional experience in ways no other species can. The powerhouse of our rational thinking, the 'cerebral cortex', has increased in size over time and is larger and more developed than in any other animal. With its higher order cognitive functioning, it can play a prominent role in the conscious interpretation and regulation of emotions. The human ability to achieve a raised level of consciousness is an incredible and empowering gift for us as a species.

Conscious leadership will drive you to use your powers of awareness to think and act with self-empowerment, integrity, kindness, empathy, inclusion and always ensure you're responsible and accountable. Your level of consciousness will also feed into the energy you bring as a leader.

Thinking and energy

As a leader, your self-talk will influence your energy levels. Your energy is super critical in the way you lead and relate to your people.

In 2006, I was a senior manager at Experian and I was aware there were going to be some big changes resulting in redundancies. I couldn't share this, but it was a continual source of *negative self-talk* for me. One of my colleagues pointed out to me that my energy and demeanour was being picked up by my team. My energy was feeding the *group behaviour*. It was a memorable piece of learning and I knew, until there was actual news to deliver, I owed it to my team to bring more positive energy.

As a leader you send out ripples in the water continuously and it will be better for you and your people to have these as positive ripples. This is where I have some challenges with the term 'authentic leadership'. It's important to be honest, consistent and vulnerable but it's also important to take responsibility for how your energy will impact the mindset and thinking of others. This means being open is not always the best choice.

'The Pygmalion Effect' is a startling example of the impact of leaders' energy.

The Pygmalion Effect

A famous study 'Pygmalion in the Classroom' was carried out by Robert Rosenthal and Lenore Jacobson in 1968. The results provide a fascinating view of the powerful effect expectations can have on performance. Intelligence tests were administered to a group of elementary school students. The researchers then told the teachers which of their students had demonstrated the greatest academic potential. However, there was a catch. The students identified by the researchers had been selected at random, not on any real indicators of intelligence. By the end of the experiment, the randomly selected students had, in fact, turned into the academic leaders of their class! Even though the teachers had been instructed not to say anything directly to the students and not to spend any extra time with them, the students flagged as having most potential had still excelled to the top of their class. The belief the teachers had in the students' potential had been unwittingly and nonverbally communicated and had been transformed into reality.

Never doubt as a leader, your mindset and your resulting energy will impact your people significantly.

The mind-traps leaders face with negative self-talk

Our *negative self-talk,* driven by our underlying *survival psychology*, can take hold speedily and wreak havoc. Here are some examples from leaders I've spoken to:

- *Negative self-talk* being common and needing constant management
- Going into spiralling self-talk which escalates and catastrophises events
- Struggling to switch off and stop thinking about the endless task list
- Being gripped by pessimism which looks for and sees the worst

These are just a small sample of the detrimental impacts of *negative self-talk* on leaders. You will certainly have your own experiences, possibly on a daily basis.

As a further example of this, I spoke to an entrepreneur recently and he talked about when he owned his own business. He said whenever the phone went, he feared it was their biggest client who would be serving notice on them. And when they served notice, other clients would follow, they would serve notice as well. It would end up he would lose his business, he would lose his home and his marriage would be lost through all this as well!

It's the elephant in the room that we can all go through these kinds of spiralling thought processes often (see my TEDx talk 'Unleashing Your Creativity By Escaping Your Survival Thinking' and the story of my reaction to losing a tooth on YouTube). It's out of control survival thinking. It can block our potential to think rationally and it narrows our focus. It can also impact on our health.

The physical impact on leaders

According to a survey by FreeAgent in 2021, more than half of UK SME owners polled said they have experienced burnout since the start of the pandemic in 2020, which equates to around 2.9 million business owners across the UK suffering from burnout. Anxiety, stress, depression and other related illnesses account for 439,000 workdays lost in the UK each year (as I shared in the introduction).

The impact of *negative self-talk* and mindset is very real in a broad sense. For us individually, it can be the physical challenges we face, as mentioned in relation to the work of Joseph Ledoux showing how our brain and nervous system are impacted by threats and danger. Over a prolonged period, the more ways we have to handle stress or pessimistic thoughts, the greater the impact will be on our mental health and wellbeing.

Characteristics and biases associated with negative self-talk

There are a number of characteristics, cognitive biases (also know as heuristics or brain shortcut) and cognitive distortions which can trap you or trip you up in your role as a leader, as they feed into the stress described.

Here are some examples:

Confirmation bias	We look for confirmation of our own pre-existing negative beliefs about ourselves. We tend to focus on evidence which supports this negative self-perception and dismiss evidence to the contrary. This was a feature in the chapters on *impostor syndrome* and *ego*. Note Confirmation bias can also confirm pre-conceived positive views too.
All or nothing thinking	People with a more negative mindset often view themselves and experiences in an 'all or nothing' fashion.
Over generalisation	We draw sweeping conclusions about ourselves, where a single or small mistake can lead us to believing we're a failure.

Self-criticism	*Negative self-talk* will often involve self-criticism and self-blame. We can continually criticise ourselves for perceived mistakes, weaknesses and shortcomings. *Negative self-talk* can also erode our self-esteem, our self-confidence, and it can damage our self-worth.
Self-limiting beliefs	*Negative self-talk* is often rooted in these kinds of beliefs and distorted thinking patterns. It leads to us making overly negative judgments about ourselves.
Magnification and minimisation	We can tend to magnify perceived faults and minimise achievements (and this is a definite feature of *impostor syndrome* too). Being impacted by this cognitive distortion can lead to a very much skewed view of our self.
Catastrophise	Negative self-talk can involve the tendency to imagine the worst possible outcomes or consequences, leading to high levels of anxiety, which are experienced by so many business leaders across the globe.

Negative labelling	Language is incredibly powerful and we can be far too quick to call ourselves a failure or unlikable.

Your awareness of going into any of these modes of thinking will be a good start. Labelling them also brings a level of detachment – "oh I see I'm catastrophising this situation too much". It will help to find calm (externally and internally), to be more rational and analytical to look at the real evidence which negates the more pessimistic ways of thinking about self. An evidence-based approach is part of Cognitive Behavioural Therapy (covered further in the solutions section).

If you find you're a victim of one or more of the above on a regular basis and struggle to gain a sense of rationality, it's important to seek expert advice.

Overcooking the need for security

The next challenge is that we can overcook the need for security, in terms of our current leadership position, future career path and financial goals.

Our *survival psychology* will very much influence this through its need for safety and its fear of potential adversity.

It can cause problems with anxiety, procrastination or keep us locked in our current place, for fear of making risky decisions or moves.

Ironically our over-inflated need for security can result in thoughts and feelings of instability and, as we know, this can impact on the results we achieve.

How to escape the mind-traps created by Negative Self-Talk

* Mindset

The most important thing we can do is to remain aware. Eckhart Tolle said in his book 'New Earth': "Thinking without awareness is the main dilemma of human existence". I believe this statement is profoundly true.

One of the most impactful concepts for me has been to remember to be 'The Watcher'. This is referenced in Eckhart Tolle's work, but the idea of 'watching the watcher' derives from Buddhism. Knowing you have the ability to be able to consciously observe your own thinking and observation, not only detaches you from this thinking but it gives you greater power to make mindful choices in how you want to think and what you want to do. This is a higher power we are blessed with as a species!

An important point

If you're finding your battle with your *negative self-talk* too debilitating don't hesitate to seek help from your GP, a therapist or counsellor.

* Practical tools and actions for you

Here are a number of practical tools and actions which will support you in relation to *negative self-talk*. Select the 1 or 2 you feel addresses your biggest challenges and focus on these first.

a) Take care of your brain as your foundation

Your brain is an organ, not an abstract concept. It needs NEWS and not the kind of daily news you're fed by newspapers and TV! It needs Nutrition, Exercise, Water and Sleep. The quality of your thinking will be directly influenced by how you look after your brain.

I see so many leaders who neglect one or more of those areas and it impacts on performance. Get back to the basics and attend to those 4 areas to look after your brain as you would the rest of your body.

b) Assess potential threats rationally

As I described earlier, your *survival psychology* will exaggerate, distort and imagine threats. It can hijack you and block your ability to think clearly and make decisions in your leadership role. When you find this happening, take 3 steps to shift your thinking and move from a state of reactivity.

Firstly, find some quiet and space, both physically and psychologically. This may mean going outside or moving somewhere different. It may mean doing some deep breathing to become present. This will slow down the frequency of the brain (we're more creative when our frequency is slowed down to 8-12 Hz which is known as 'alpha frequency').

Secondly, assess the threat calmly. This is a chance to minimise the impact of your *survival psychology*. Seek out data and facts to analyse, which will both enable you to move out of your negative perspective and allow you to think based on objectivity. Look at your possible solutions and ways forward and weigh up the potential risks.

Thirdly, make conscious choices and move forwards in the best way for you at this moment.

You need a pattern interrupt to take yourself out of the hijacking and engage the logical part of the brain (the cerebral cortex) and these 3 steps will help you do this.

c) Be your own best coach or seek a coach

The next solution is to be your best coach, rather than your worst critic. Have constructive conversations with yourself as you would do with a colleague or somebody in your team who needs your support.

Coach yourself to make better choices and act based on those. You can support this by moving from an inner monologue to a dialogue. Have a conversation with your own self-talk and challenge it when it becomes negative or pessimistic.

Here is an example of the kind of conversation I have with myself:

"It's going to be a disaster!!"……….

> "Oh I see why you're seeing things this way, but let me help you to see it differently"
> "What would happen if the oppositive were to be the case?"
> "If the worst were to happen what would really be the impact?"
> "How can you mitigate against this?"

Have better dialogues with yourself, rather than getting hooked into a spiralling monologue. Doing this will give you an upper hand in the battle between your 'potential self' and 'destructive self'.

If you find this too challenging and can't see the wood for the trees, it may well be worth seeking a coach who can support you in handling this and realising more of your potential.

d) Be consciously vigilant of the words you use

Your words will have an impact on others and critically they will effect your thinking and perspectives. Notice when you have moved to more negative or doubtful language (as I described earlier) and shift this speedily:

- You're not going to "try" you're going to "do".
- You "can" rather than "can't".
- This is not a "disaster" it is a "problem".

Choose more empowering words within your self-talk and the way you express yourself to people in your organisation.

e) If things appear overwhelming, focus on the manageable

Overwhelm will be a fertile feeding ground for *negative self-talk* and it's a very common experience for leaders juggling a whole myriad of balls! Identify the small steps you can take which are within your control and keep building from there.

Whether the overwhelm is due to perceived adversity or the real volume of stuff you have to do, it's important to step back and assess what you can do first. You can build a plan, but focus on taking the next step because your self-empowerment will be very much impacted by action.

Celebrate the small wins as you move forwards too as this will support your momentum (more about celebration shortly).

f) Reframe your perspective and move from pessimism to optimism

Reframe your view of events and people by shifting your thinking. Notice when you have slipped into any one of the 4 traps of pessimism and coach yourself to move to the more optimistic side.

If you find one of the cognitive biases or other characteristics of *negative self-talk* take hold of you, immediately look to change you thinking and shift your perspective. How can you see this (or you) differently and in a more positive way? Reframe your view of yourself, the people around you or your organisation to see things in a more supportive and helpful way.

g) Capture and celebrate the good things

On the path to making yourself a more optimistic person, the simple act of writing down 5 positive things about each day will change the way you focus on your experiences. It is a very simple example of the 'Tetris Effect' being used to see positive patterns.

I started doing this in 2013 and persist with it to this very day. It has made me more optimistic in my outlook. For you, it will start to change the way you think about and see your world. Rather than looking for problems, threats, things which haven't been done or things which have gone wrong, your monitoring radar will see the good more and the things you and your team are achieving. By continually doing this habitually, it will change your view of yourself and your view of the world around you to be a more optimistic person in nature. Changing your thinking and how you see things will change what you do ('think see do'). It will change your results too.

In a broader sense, celebrate the good more. Celebrate it individually, but also celebrate it collectively with your teams. Talk about wins in meetings, newsletters, on intranets, at reviews. Spend quality time sharing the positives and learn from these too.

h) Work on increasing your positivity ratio

Take the advice of psychologists like Fredrickson and Losada. Flip your positive experiences and emotions so you move yourself to a stronger ratio of good to bad, both for your own internal experiences and the way you lead others too.

Fredrickson is a proponent of ensuring we consciously have more positive emotions. In her view 3:1 is the ratio to aim for.

She also developed her 'Broaden and Build Theory' in 1998, which proposes how positive emotions broaden our mental horizons enabling us to see more possibilities.

A further example of the 3:1 ratio runs through the work of psychologist Marciel Losada (as touched on previously). In his research across 60 organisations, he found a ratio of at least 3:1 (up to 6:1) of positive feedback from leaders, as opposed to more critical feedback, is where a team's performance improves consistently.

For yourself, savour those micro moments where you experience positive feelings, as these will provide a buffer against stress and improve your mental health and wellbeing. Spend more time fully appreciating why those moments are special and enjoy the richness of those experiences and the reflection.

For others, give more positive feedback and appreciation on a regular basis. It will make you feel good and them too and, as we saw with 'The Pygmalion Effect', it will improve performance.

i) Use evidence-based approaches like Cognitive Behavioural Therapy (CBT)

You can also employ the approaches of CBT (or be supported by a therapist in doing this). In this therapeutical approach, evidence is used to challenge negative thinking, *negative self-talk* and negative beliefs. It means when you get sucked into one of those areas, you challenge the evidence supporting the negativity and look for evidence to shift to a more positive outlook or thinking. It's a useful technique to combat *impostor syndrome* too.

j) Mindfulness and meditation

You can also look into the areas of mindfulness, meditation and breathing techniques to free yourself from the endless spiral of self-talk which goes on via those 1000s of thoughts you have every day.

Meditation can give you some quality space and time. Just focusing on deep breathing alone can take you out of your mind and bring you into a different and more peaceful state (I'm going to strongly recommend Natalie Creasy, owner of Little Soul Shack, if you would like to explore this area further).

Mindfulness is an approach to life where you enjoy experiences in a more conscious and focused way. You experience eating your food, washing up, going for a walk and other regular experiences, rather than be distracted by other things going on or the inner dialogue. Mindfulness is about being more present with your experiences rather being distracted by mobile devices or inner chatter. Mindfulness will also help you listen to your people fully, without being hijacked by the filters described earlier.

Both areas are well worth exploring for leaders who are typically gripped by busyness and an endless task list.

k) Your social world

Be mindful of your social investment and the kinds of people you spend your time with, as this will have a big impact on your psyche. In very simple terms, look to minimise time with people who are a more negative energy drain (or cut off from them completely if feasible) and increase your time with more positive people.

When you're struggling with your frame of mind and internal *negative self-talk*, speaking to others you trust will almost inevitably have a positive impact on this. Reach out if you're struggling because the people who care about you will want to be there for you.

l) Keep your sense of humour

When perceived adversity strikes and *negative self-talk* takes hold, do your very best to use one of the 24 identified character strengths (from Martin Seligman). See the funny side!

Humour (used carefully and kindly) can take the heat out of a 'fight flight freeze' moment. It can be a pattern interrupt and take you away from the perceived threat and the grip of your *survival psychology*. Humour will also put your brain in a more positive state (through the release of Dopamine – the mere act of smiling can release this) and will fuel your problem-solving capability.

m) Your purpose and strengths

Look at the purpose for your work and have a strong personal purpose too. Your commitment in both aspects will drive you through the challenges you experience and the strength of your purpose and conviction will shape your thinking around these.

On your journey, look to do more things which utilise your strengths, as this will bolster your self-esteem. This is a core principle of the positive psychology movement. Where you believe you are less strong, look to work with others who are strong in these areas, either for them to do the things you can't or to educate you.

n) Your habitual thinking and behaviour

Finally, remember your habitual behaviour and thinking can be changed and you can frequently rewire your neurology through repetition.

Do the things which put you in a more positive state. It could be listening to music, going out for a walk, having time with your family, having time with your pets, doing some reading, watching an enjoyable film. Do the things which you know feed your mind in a more positive way and manage the things which don't.

Look at your regular habits, in terms of how you feed your mind and make conscious choices to shift your habits. It might mean reducing your time spent watching the news (for all the reasons I covered earlier), less alcohol and less social media scrolling. It may also mean spending more time exercising regularly, having time out in nature or reading a book.

Summary

- We have thousands of thoughts every day, the majority of which are doubtful or negative in nature. This can lead us to become captured by spiraling *negative self-talk* that will impact on our mindset, energy, decision-making and actions

- We are wired to be more pessimistic, this is believed to have been the case since the 'Iron Age', and will continually have our survival radar set to look for threats and potential adversity

- We are the only species believed to have the ability to consciously rise above our own thinking, observe it and either ignore or shift it. This is our superpower!

- We can build in habitual behaviours that will rewire our neurology and change our thinking patterns. This can make us more positive and optimistic in nature.

We have been on a journey through all 5 areas of *survival psychology* and the mind-traps which can hijack you as a leader. We've also looked at the many ways you can become aware of these and escape them, enabling you to realise more of your potential. Let's move onto some final thoughts.

CONCLUSION

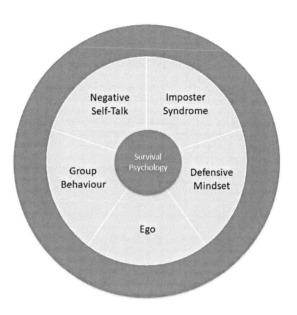

"Escaping the mind-traps of survival thinking."

I leave you with some final thoughts

We've examined the concept of *survival psychology* and I trust this has now raised your awareness of how it can manifest for you via the mind-traps in those 5 different areas.

You have a whole raft of tools and approaches to help you '*escape the mind-traps of survival thinking*'. My recommendation would be to start with the area you feel most challenged with and then pick a couple of tools from that section to consciously work on.

The more you raise your conscious awareness of what is going on internally for you, the greater personal power and control you will have.

The human brain is an incredible and complex organ and human psychology can be complicated too (the volumes of books, research and theories give testament to this!). However, the way we think can also be incredibly basic.

We all have a driving survival instinct which will kick in when we're faced with scenarios where we feel threatened. It is vital to our physical survival, but in modern life we are very much focused on internal threats and our psychological survival too. We go inwards and look for vulnerability and weaknesses. We are on the alert for threats to our self-esteem, happiness and practical safety.

If we go back to that hall of mirrors in Edinburgh in 2022, my daughter and I had a lot of fun seeing our images be exaggerated, distorted and completely transformed. Our *survival psychology* impacts us all and it can exaggerate, distort and imagine threats. This is no fun at all. When it works well, it is a fundamental to keeping us safe. Unfortunately, it can often be irrational and when it goes inward it can often leave us feeling 'not good enough' in various parts of our lives and work.

It's vital for you to become conscious and aware when your *survival psychology* strikes with one of its many mind-traps so you can escape these via shifting your thinking and perspectives. Becoming more conscious of what is going on, finding some calm headspace and observing your thinking, gives you greater power. It lessens the grip of your more destructive thinking. It gives you greater power to think different and shift your perspective to see your situation differently. Then importantly, you can act in different ways and get better results.

As I've said throughout, it's not a matter of "feeling the fear and doing it anyway". It's about understanding the fear first!

Take good care of your brain too. It's a physical organ and as in the *negative self-talk* chapter it needs NEWS (Nutrition, Exercise, Water and Sleep). Don't overcomplicate things if you're experiencing psychological challenges, start with the basics first. To be able to manage your *survival psychology,* you need your brain to be in optimum condition.

It is however, critically important that, if you're struggling to shift your thinking and you're battling with deeper rooted mental health issues, you seek help speedily.

See your doctor or contact an organisation such as https://www.mind.org.uk or https://www.nhs.uk/nhs-services/mental-health-services)

As a leader (and a caring human being), it's also your responsibility to keep a watchful eye on the people close to you – your team, your family and your friends. Help them see how their *survival psychology* is impacting on their behaviour and performance. Do your best to do this in a supportive and non-accusatory way too.

I trust you have found *survival psychology* and the 5 areas of my model a fascinating topic to explore. We're all familiar with our survival instinct, but it may well be the case you hadn't realised quite how much it's playing out in your modern life. Being more aware of it, managing it and escaping its *mind-traps* is going to be fundamental to your growth as a leader and human being. It will help you see that perceived 'Sabre-Toothed Tigers' are really only small or non-existent problems.

We all experience survival thinking which can constrain our potential, but it's normal and we can overcome it to become the leader and person we are truly capable of being.

Further help

Podcast Show

My podcast show 'Leadership Mindset' has been on air since 2018, with a whole range of fascinating interviews (some of which have been referred to during the book) and solo episodes.

You can find it here – www.leadershipmindset.co.uk and it is available on Spotify, Stitcher and Apple (search for Leadership Mindset Tony Brooks)

LinkedIn

I regularly post on LinkedIn about different aspects of *survival psychology* and how it plays out for leaders. This includes the feeling of not being good enough, perfectionism, *impostor syndrome, defensive mindset, negative self-talk, ego* and *group behaviour*.

Feel free to check out my LinkedIn profile and connect. I'm really interested to get your feedback and your thoughts on how you relate to the concept of *survival psychology* and how you see it impacting you or how you have seen it impact other people, so comments and questions on the posts would be appreciated.

Connect with me here – www.linkedin.com/in/tonybrooks63

Websites

My company website –
www.theleadershiptrainingworkshop.com

My personal website – www.thetonybrooks.com

Next steps

If you would like help with challenges you are having in any of the 5 areas in this book or feel they are blocking your potential growth as a leader, drop me a line at:

tony@thetonybrooks.com

Or connect and DM me on LinkedIn at

www.linkedin.com/in/tonybrooks63

Looking for a speaker for your event?

Tony speaks in person and online on his main keynote: **'Survival Psychology – How Leaders Can Escape The Mind-Traps of Survival Thinking'**

Key takeaways from Tony's talk

1. Why you may think you have **Impostor Syndrome**, but you don't!

2. How to handle mistakes, challenges and feedback to move out of a **Defensive Mindset** and enable you to grow

3. Why we are wired for pessimism and **Negative Self-Talk**, but how being conscious will be your superpower

4. How to overcome the 3 Cs of **Ego** (Competing, Complaining and Criticising)

5. How to shift **Group Behaviour** from being divisive to being a power for good

All 5 of these areas are also provided as deep-dive talks in their own right

You can find out more about Tony's work as a speaker and key takeaways for your audience from his talks at – www.thetonybrooks.com/speaking

A range of resources, videos and brochures for speaker bookers and agents can be found at – www.thetonybrooks.com/pr-speaker-resources

Tony is a registered speaker with these agencies

Raise the Bar – www.raisethebar.co.uk/speaker/tony-brooks

Champions – www.champions-speakers.co.uk/speaker-agent/tony-brooks

"It is without doubt Tony will leave you wanting 'more'. An inspirational speaker I was truly captivated by his presentation on Survival Psychology. He is honest, intuitive, personable and exceptionally credible." - **Annie Leaver, CFCIPD**

"I recently had the opportunity to experience Tony's talk on survival psychology with a group of fellow HR professionals. I don't say this lightly when I say it was the best 90minutes I've spent at work for some time. Tony's session was informative, thought provoking and challenging in equal measure." - **Darren Jones, Instinct HR**

My TEDx talk

On January 18th 2024 I brought some of the concepts in this book to life in a TEDx talk called 'Unleashing Your Creativity By Escaping Your Survival Thinking'.

You will be able to find this on the 'TEDx Talks' YouTube channel.

Here are examples of the feedback I received from attendees:

"You absolutely nailed it!! Such an inspiration and such a powerful message that I really needed to hear today" - **Donna Smith, Coach for Lawyers**

"Tony delivered with such passion and enthusiasm, and he left me hanging onto every word. I wanted to write down every bit of wisdom immediately!" - **Beth Bearder, Employment Lawyer**

"You really were phenomenal. You were fantastic, your talk was incredible and I would go so far to say it was like faultless!" - **Charlie Whyman, Professional Speaking Association President**

"Tony's knack for bringing psychology to life is just extraordinary! His stories, especially the one about his teeth, cleverly connected to the fear symbolised by a Sabre-Toothed Tiger, were both enlightening and entertaining" - **Pete Colby, Director Pragmatism Mediation**

"Most people say they would rather die than do public speaking. Witnessing Tony Brooks deliver his TEDx talk, it was clear that he felt the opposite. He'd rather do public speaking than die. What a speaker! What a speech!" - **Claudia Crawley, Executive Coach**

"You were incredible Tony – best of the day! So calm, confident, funny, engaging and with clear messaging" – **Pam Burrows, Professional Speaker**

Your help

If you have found the book an interesting and useful read, I would really appreciate one of the following:

- A review on Amazon
- A recommendation on LinkedIn
- A testimonial which you can email to tony@thetonybrooks.com

Or just drop me a line and let me know what you thought of the book 😊

If you know of other leaders who would benefit from reading this, please recommend they get a copy or pass on yours.

Thank you again for investing your money and time in my book.

Bibliography

- Leadership Is Language – Lt. David Marquet
- 5 Dysfunctions Of A Team – Patrick Lencioni
- Emotional Intelligence – Daniel Goleman
- The New Leaders – Daniel Goleman
- New Earth – Eckhart Tolle
- Learned Optimism - Dr. Martin Seligman
- Authentic Happiness - Dr. Martin Seligman
- Flourish - Dr. Martin Seligman
- Imposter Cure – Dr. Jessamy Hibberd
- Happiness Advantage – Shaun Achor
- Brain Is Boss – Dr. Lynda Shaw
- Ego Is The Enemy – Ryan Holiday
- Positivity - Barbara Fredrickson
- Leadership Mindset 2.0 – R. Michael Anderson
- Excuses Begone Wayne Dyer
- I'm Ok, You're OK – Thomas A. Harris
- Positive Psychology In Business – Sarah Lewis
- Mindset – Dr. Carol S. Dweck
- Anxious – Joseph LeDoux

- Borderline, Narcissistic & Schizoid Adaptions – Dr, Elinor Greenberg
- Tribes – Seth Godin
- Tribal Leadership - Dave Logan, Halee Fischer-Wright & John King
- Legacy – James Kerr
- Engaged – Amy Brann
- Selected – Mark van Vugt
- Rainy Brain, Sunny Brain – Elaine Fox
- Your Survival Instinct IS Killing Me
- Evolutionary Psychology – Robin Dunbar, John Lycett & Lousie Barrett